BRITISH MALAYA

THEMES IN EUROPEAN EXPANSION: EXPLORATION,
COLONIZATION, AND THE IMPACT OF EMPIRE
(General Editor: James A. Casada)
Vol. 1

GARLAND REFERENCE LIBRARY
OF SOCIAL SCIENCE
Vol. 79

BRITISH MALAYA
A Bibliographical and
Biographical Compendium

Robert Heussler

GARLAND PUBLISHING, INC. • NEW YORK & LONDON
1981

Library of Congress Cataloging in Publication Data

Heussler, Robert.
  British Malaya.

  (Themes in European Expansion ; v. 1)
(Garland reference library of social science ; v. 79)
  Includes index.
    1. Malaya—Bibliography.   2. Malaya—Biography.
I. Title.   II. Series.
Z3246.H48 [DS592]   016.9595'1   80-8968
ISBN 0-8240-9369-0   AACR2

Printed on acid-free, 250-year-life paper
Manufactured in the United States of America

to
The Malayan Civil Service

CONTENTS

EDITOR'S INTRODUCTION

It is quite appropriate that Robert Heussler's *British Malaya: A Bibliographical and Biographical Compendium* should launch the series "Themes in European Expansion: Exploration, Colonization, and the Impact of Empire." This work is the latest of many publications by one of the most productive scholars presently writing on the history of British imperial expansion. Like all of the author's studies, the book is the product of meticulous scholarship. Moreover, it admirably achieves the general aim of the series which it inaugurates—to provide useful tools of scholarly reference which combine traditional approaches and innovative techniques to fill significant gaps in the existing literature in their respective fields.

Heussler, who presently is Professor of History at the State University of New York, College at Geneseo, received his undergraduate degree at Dartmouth in 1948. Variegated academic training, including study at the College of Chinese Studies, Peking; at the Woodrow Wilson School of Public and International Affairs, Princeton University; and at St. Antony's College, Oxford, followed. The author received his doctorate from Princeton in 1961. He has had extensive experience in academic and professional positions, and these endeavors have given him wide exposure on an international level. Among the positions Heussler has held are those of overseas representative for Lowell Thomas (in this capacity he visited over 150 countries), work in the Ford Foundation's Latin American program, and a stint as president of Trenton State College. In addition, he has been the recipient of numerous honors, fellowships, and grants. A tireless and productive researcher, Heussler's major scholarly works include: *Yesterday's Rulers: The Making of the British Colonial Service* (1963); *The British in Northern Nigeria* (1968); *British Tanganyika* (1971); and *Rulers of British Malaya: The Malayan Civil Service and Its Predecessors, 1867–1942* (1981).

The present volume marks the culmination of a decade of intensive specialized research on British imperial activities in Malaya. In a broader sense, it is the latest outgrowth of the lifetime of scholarly activity Heussler has devoted to enhancing our understanding of the men and methods that were the backbone of the splendid imperial edifice which was the British Empire. In this work the author provides a detailed guide to the personnel of the Malayan Civil Service from the inception of Colonial Office responsibility for the region in 1867 to the Japanese conquest in 1942.

Each administrative official who served in Malaya during this era is covered by a solid biographical sketch which delineates the major known features of his career. These sketches, which include all available information bearing on every facet of the officials' backgrounds and activities, collectively constitute a "who's who" of the British in Malaya. They are based on research in a wide array of manuscript and printed sources, including many that are still closed to the general public. The biographical entries are nicely complemented by an extensive bibliography which becomes the standard source on the subject. The latter portion of the work will be invaluable to anyone interested in more general developments in nineteenth- and twentieth-century Malaya. It updates and in many ways, particularly as regards the individuals covered in the biographical section, supersedes H.A.R. Cheeseman's *Bibliography of Malaya* (1959). Careful indexing and appropriate comment and cross-referencing also add to the work's utility.

Taken as a whole, Heussler's book should be recognized as a welcome application of a prosopographical approach to the creation of a vital reference tool. It will be a work of value to scholars and specialists in a number of fields and disciplines. It is a major contribution to British imperial history as well as that of Southeast Asia, it provides much-needed biographical information on hundreds of individuals (both prominent and those largely ignored by posterity), and it marks a new departure in the bio-bibliographical technique of research.

James A. Casada, *Series Editor*
Winthrop College

ACKNOWLEDGMENTS

I owe a very large debt of gratitude to Sir William Goode and his colleagues of the Malayan Civil Service who generously helped with the gathering of biographical details which are not available in civil lists. In Malaysia, Tan Sri Mubin Sheppard kindly supplied information on Malay officers of the pre–1941 generation and on many books and articles. I thank the staff members of the principal libraries and archives where I have worked over the past ten years, notably the Malaysian National Archives, the Singapore National Archives, the Public Record Office, London, the Royal Commonwealth Society Library, the India Office Library, and the libraries of the University of Malaya, Cornell University, Yale University, Columbia University, London University, Dartmouth College and Oxford University.

It is a pleasure to have this opportunity of recording special appreciation to F.E. Leese, librarian of Rhodes House, Oxford, Mrs. M.C. Crawford of the Wason Collection office at Cornell, Peter A. Crowther of the Brynmor Jones Library at the University of Hull and William Lane of the Milne Library, State University of New York, College at Geneseo.

PREFACE

As the immediate post-war phase of Asian and African nationalism recedes further into the past, and with it much of the emotional anti-colonialism that has marked recent scholarship on that era, there has been a revival of interest in the records of European powers in tropical areas. Whatever they may think about the rights and wrongs of alien rule, many specialists have come to feel that new states and their problems cannot be understood without reference to the European background. Influence from abroad is seen to have been great, not only in the obvious fields of politics and economic development, but more profoundly and lastingly in the assumptions and processes of thought that came from outside and that linger on after the flags of independence have been run up.

The contributions of British administration and scholarship to the building of modern Malaysia are especially noteworthy in view of the primitive state of local polities before the colonial period and the comparatively long tenure of the Europeans in that part of the world. Captain Francis Light of the East India Company established himself at Penang in 1786, and the last of his successors did not depart until 1957. In the interim the British not only made a nation; in addition, as Sir Richard Winstedt observed, they taught the Malays their history and realigned languages and literature to answer the complicated demands of modern commerce and education.[1]

A substantial proportion of the writing on Malaya over the past two centuries has been done by scholar-administrators. Students of colonial government in Southeast Asia and elsewhere will not find this surprising. Whether or not they object to the

---

[1]See H.A.R. Cheeseman, *Bibliography of Malaya* (London: Longmans, 1959), p. vii.

points of view encountered in the various works, most will rec-
ognize their value and will continue to make use of them.[2] In so
doing they will be aware of the reasons for the phenomenon and
will not think it reprehensible. Indeed, there are those who re-
gret the growing separation between public affairs and literary
pursuits, a nineteenth-century trend that was deplored by reflec-
tive people at the time and still is today. If the writings of
Thucydides and Milton, of Goethe and Macaulay, were the more
valuable for the practical experience that underlay their judg-
ments and enriched their exposition, then perhaps students of
Malayan history are not wrong to see advantages in McNair's
long service as an engineer and superintendent of prisons and in
Pickering's apprenticeship before the mast and his years with a
commercial firm on the China coast.

Not every civil servant devotes his spare time to writing.
Why, we may ask, did so many in British Malaya put their
thoughts and observations on paper and publish them for others
to read? The answers were doubtless as many and varied as the
officers themselves, but the circumstances of their careers were
similar and these provide a common denominator. The majority
were educated men, that is, they had been exposed to the great
tradition of humanistic studies that formed the basis of curricula
in the nineteenth- and twentieth-century schools and universities of their country. The high standards of such institutions and
the cultural homogeneity of the society which they functioned in
account in no small part for the literacy and the articulate assur-
ance of the British, especially in the exotic situations of the
tropics where they exercised authority for so many generations.
On this foundation of capability and self-confidence they built
durable structures of local knowledge. They knew languages,
not as students, but as participants soaked in the atmosphere
that the foreign tongues were part of. The impressions they
recorded about the way people lived and how they thought came
from everyday experience of the most mundane and therefore

[2] See W. David MacIntyre, "Malaya from the 1850's to the 1870's, and Its Histori-
ans, 1950–1970: From Strategy to Sociology" in C.D. Cowan and O.W. Wolters,
eds., *Southeast Asian History and Historiography* (Ithaca: Cornell University Press,
1976), pp. 262–284.

the most authentic kind. When they wrote of social organization or governmental forms they fashioned their designs in the light of their own sweated labor on the ground, not from anthropological checklists drawn up by abstract theorists of the universal. Though they worked hard—the best of them were never really off duty—officers had more time to come to know their people than ethnographers can normally afford. The very fact of living alongside the communities they wrote about during careers of thirty years or more gave them an intimacy of access that few professional scholars can hope to achieve. Moreover, the administrator had an interest in his subject that was unusually intense and compelling. It was his life work, no more, no less, and this resulted in strong emotional and intellectual commitment. If he lacked formal training in research and the cool detachment of the academic, such shortcomings were balanced by knowledge and understanding that were both broad and deep.

The extraordinary functional and geographical scope of their career activities gives a special pertinence to the books and articles of civil servants. This bibliography contains works by members of branches other than the Malayan Civil Service (MCS)—education, legal, public works, police, medical, customs, agriculture, forestry—but even within the MCS itself there was a wide range. The mainstream of the service, the Malay-speaking one, dealt with land office management, district administration and secretariat functions as well as relations with planters and miners, while the men of the so-called Chinese Protectorate addressed themselves to the multifarious occupations of the country's largest immigrant community and the Labor Department to workers pouring into Malaya from India. Beyond the peninsula were the Borneo territories, various island groups, occasionally an enclave or two in China and some of the outlying domains of the king of Siam. By the early years of the twentieth century Malaya had become an administrative mother hen, supplying senior officers to other dependencies of the colonial empire. And soon after the United States acquired the Philippines Washington asked for and got detailed advice from the MCS on methods of dealing with overseas possessions. The importance of the service and the relevance of its story therefore are by no means confined to the small country, roughly the size of England, that was its main concern.

Nor did the spirit and style of British government cease when independence came. A remarkable continuity of outlook and technique links the writings and comments of retired Europeans on the one hand and their Malay contemporaries and successors on the other.[3] The autobiography of Sir Mahmud bin Mat bears ample testimony to this as do the verbal remarks of Othman bin Mohamed and any number of Malay district officers who were schoolboys when the British left and with whom one discussed present-day administrative problems in their headquarters as recently as the mid–1970s. Independence came about through friendly negotiation, not violence and revolution as in neighboring Indonesia and Indo-China. The stamp of British attitudes and methods, still in evidence today, is a clear indication that interracial government worked well and that the modernizing efforts of the MCS were appreciated.

This bibliography focuses on the period from 1867, when London took over the straits settlements, to 1942, the year of the Japanese conquest, although considerable attention is given to the pre-colonial and post–1945 years as well. Shortly after assuming direct control of the colony, which had been ruled from India for over eighty years, Britain expanded its holdings on the mainland of Malaya, mainly to stop the internecine warfare among Chinese mining groups that was damaging trade. Then began the economic build-up that eventually made Malaya the most valuable of all the British colonies. Based at the outset on "country trade"—tin, pepper, gambier, gutta percha, coffee— and on the entrepôt business of Singapore, it reached unprecedented heights after the turn of the century when rubber became the most profitable export. All this was sustained by the highly successful combination of British management and imported labor, first Chinese and later, on a smaller scale, Indian. Works listed in section VI trace the course of these developments and identify problems of social indigestion flowing from a

---

[3] In recognizing this continuity and documenting it James C. Scott is rather critical, viewing it as a reactionary force. See his *Political Ideology in Malaysia: Reality and the Beliefs of an Elite* (New Haven: Yale University Press, 1968).

massive immigration that assumed an indefinite prolongation of British rule. Given the economic boom and the absence of nationalism, however, it is not to be wondered at that a sense of timeless well-being continued straight through to the outbreak of World War II.

Japan's administration lasted only a short time, 1942–1945. But a return to the prosperity of the pre-war years was delayed by the Chinese communist insurrection, the "emergency" that began in 1948 and lasted into the late 1950s. With the celebration of independence in 1957 the colonial period came to a close.

This volume is designed to provide sources for an overview of the main themes and historical developments of the British phase in Malaya's history, together with biographical sketches of the men who bore the burden of responsibility for supervising trade and government.

Part One
Bibliography

PART ONE
Bibliography

The following lists are selective. They aim at a representative
treatment of the historical development of Malaya in the British
years: land, society, culture, economy and government. In the
cases of prolific scholars such as Sir Richard Winstedt, only
small numbers of especially significant works are included. All
principal elements of the population are represented: aboriginal,
Malay, Chinese, Indian and European. In addition to works about
the various groups, the lists also contain studies by members
of each group and by others such as Americans, Japanese, French
and Dutch. Annotation varies from comparative fullness for
particularly important works to shorter comments on others and
none when titles and/or sub-titles are adequately descriptive.

Abbreviations and Symbols

HMSO:	Her Majesty's Stationery Office
(M):	Personal papers of retired civil servants, to be deposited in Rhodes House, Oxford
MCS:	Malayan Civil Service
SBRAS:	Journal of the Straits Branch of the Royal Asiatic Society, 1878 to November 1922
JMBRAS:	Journal of the Malayan (later Malaysian) Branch of the Royal Asiatic Society, from 1922 onward
*	An asterisk before the name of an author indicates that a biographical entry will be found in Part Two.

I. BIBLIOGRAPHIES AND DIRECTORIES

1. Cheeseman, H.A.R. *Bibliography of Malaya*. London: Longmans, 1959. Pp. 234.

    Assembled by a member of the government service. Helpfully categorized and reasonably complete for the time period, though erratic in detail. Not fully annotated.

2. Hellman, Florence S. *British Malaya and British North Borneo: A Bibliographical List*. Washington, D.C.: Library of Congress, 1943. Pp. 103.

    Largely superseded by entry 1.

3. Lim, Beda. "Malaya, a Background Bibliography." *JMBRAS* 35:1-199.

    While not as comprehensive as entry 1, this is a useful listing, especially in the area of political history.

4. Robson, J.H.M. *A Bibliography of Malaya*. Kuala Lumpur: Caxton Press, 1941. Pp. 54.

    Largely superseded by entry 1.

5. Roff, W.R. *Bibliography of Malay and Arabic Periodicals Published in the Straits Settlements and Peninsular Malay States 1876-1941*. London: Oxford University Press, 1972. Pp. 74.

    A listing of periodicals not in English.

6. Singapore National Library. *Books About Singapore and Malaysia*. Singapore: Government Printing Office, 1965. Pp. 40.

    Less comprehensive in scope and not as full as entry 1. Designed for readers new to the subject.

7. Tregonning, K.G. *Malaysian Historical Sources*. Singapore: Department of History, University of Singapore, 1962. Pp. 130.

A historiographical listing and as such more useful than entries 1 through 6.

8. Winks, Robin W., ed. *The Historiography of the British Empire-Commonwealth: Trends, Interpretations and Resources* Durham, N.C.: Duke University Press, 1966. Pp. 596.

    Contains an excellent bibliographical essay on Malaya by C. Mary Turnbull, pp. 460-492, with citations in foot-notes. Much the most helpful of the listings in evaluation and in describing the scope of Malayan historiography to date.

II. HISTORY AND SOCIAL SCIENCE

9. Alatas, Syed Hussein. *Modernization and Social Change*.
    Sydney: Angus and Robertson, 1972. Pp. 224.

    Maintains that the British strengthened the prestige
    of the government and of the Malay aristocracy by absorbing
    the latter into the apparatus of colonial government. Also
    illuminating on advantages seized by the Chinese within the
    British system. Rejects the argument that Islam is anti-
    commercial.

10. ————. *The Myth of the Lazy Native*. London: Cass, 1977.
    Pp. 267.

    The image of the Malays, Filipinos and Javanese in the
    eyes of the Europeans from the sixteenth to the twentieth
    century and how this figures in the ideology of colonial
    capitalism. Critical of Sir Frank Swettenham and other
    leaders of British Malaya.

11. Allen, Sir Richard. *Malaysia: Prospect and Retrospect. The
    Impact and Aftermath of Colonial Rule*. New York: Oxford
    University Press, 1968. Pp. 330.

    An overview of British methods and achievements through-
    out the main periods of the colonial era and a summary of
    contemporary problems. By a fair-minded but not uncritical
    outside observer.

12. *Aston, A.V. "Review of the Sungei Manik Padi Irrigation
    Scheme." *Malayan Agricultural Journal* 28:322-329.

    First-hand account of a typical agricultural effort during
    the inter-war years as supervised by the administrative
    officer responsible for the area.

13. Bastin, John S. *The Western Element in Modern Southeast
    Asian History*. Kuala Lumpur: University of Malaya Press,
    1960. Pp. 27.

An abbreviated version of an inaugural lecture examining
European contributions to the field. Most useful as an
overview.

14.   ————, and Winks, Robin W. *Malaysia: Selected Historical
      Readings*. Kuala Lumpur: Oxford University Press, 1966.
      Pp. 484.

      Policy documents and government prints on a wide variety
      of subjects from the earliest years of British rule to
      modern times, with explanatory annotations for each selec-
      tion.

15.   *Blagden, C.O. "Notes on Malay History." *SBRAS* 53: 139-162.

      Revisionist view of Singapore and Malacca history, dis-
      puting Wilkinson and others on Malay colonization of the
      peninsula. By scholar-administrator.

16.   ————. "Siam and the Malay Peninsula." *Journal of the
      Royal Asiatic Society* 1906:107-119.

      Siam's claims in Malaya in the light of Malay history.
      The jurisdiction of China. Disputes Siam's claims which
      are considered pretentious.

17.   Braddell, Sir Roland St. J. *The Legal Status of the Malay
      States*. Singapore: Malay Publishing House, 1931. Pp. 52.

      An examination of the legal implications of the decen-
      tralization policy of Sir Cecil Clementi, by a prominent
      straits attorney and member of government commissions. A
      conservative statement by contrast with the governor's Sri
      Menanti speech looking to greater unity in Malaya.

18.   Brimmell, J.H. *Communism in Southeast Asia: A Political
      Analysis*. London: Oxford University Press for the Royal
      Institute of International Affairs, 1959. Pp. 415.

      A definitive political science treatment by a post-war
      member of the government service with considerable experi-
      ence of his subject.

19.   Brockway, Lucille H. *Science and Colonial Expansion: The
      Role of the British Royal Botanic Gardens*. New York:
      Academic Press, 1979. Pp. 240.

      Analysis of the social and political implications of
      scientific research. In Malaya the subject is seen to have
      particular relevance due to the great economic, social and
      political effects of rubber growing.

20. Buckley, C.B. *An Anecdotal History of Old Times in Singapore.* Singapore: University of Malaya Press, 1965. Pp. 790.

    A narrative account, year by year, from the early nineteenth century onwards. Personalities, trade, government. Originally a series of articles in a Singapore weekly.

21. Butcher, John. *The British in Malaya 1880-1941.* Kuala Lumpur: Oxford University Press, 1979. Pp. 300.

    Sociological treatment of selected individuals and communities. From a doctoral dissertation based on interviews in England and Malaysia and archival work. Has special reference to race relations.

22. Cameron, John. *Our Tropical Possessions in Malayan India, Being a Descriptive Account of Singapore, Penang, Province Wellesley and Malacca; Their Peoples, Products, Commerce and Government.* London: Smith Elder and Company, 1865. Pp. 408.

23. Chandran, J. "Private Enterprise and British Policy in the Malay Peninsula: The Case of the Malay and Works Construction Company, 1893-1895." *JMBRAS* 37:28-46.

    A case study in labor recruitment policy in relation to government encouragement of economic development.

24. ————. "British Foreign Policy and the Extraterritorial Question in Siam 1891-1900." *JMBRAS* 38:290-313.

    The background to Britain's agreement with Siam providing for British advisory officers in Malay states claimed by Siam. This led to the British take-over in Kedah, Kelantan, Perlis and Trengganu in 1909.

25. *Clifford, Sir Hugh. *Further India: Being the Story of Exploration from the Earliest Times in Burma, Malaya, Siam and Indo-China.* London: Alston Rivers Ltd., 1905. Pp. 378.

26. ————. *Heroes in Exile.* London: Murray, 1906. Pp. 320.

    Stories, originally printed in magazines, telling of the experiences of Europeans in the East. Written during and after the author's early service in Malaya.

27. *Corry, W.C.S. *Malaya Today.* London: Longmans, 1955, Pp. 48.

An informational booklet for general readers. By former
civil servant serving as secretary of the British Association of Malaya in London.

28.   Cowan, C.D. *Nineteenth Century Malaya: Origins of British
       Political Control*. London: Oxford University Press,
       1967. Pp. 286.

       The definitive monograph on British policy towards Malaya
       with special attention to the period from the 1860s to
       the 1890s. By the director of the School of Oriental and
       African Studies, University of London.

29.   ———, and *Wolters, O.W., eds. *Southeast Asian History
       and Historiography: Essays Presented to D.G.E. Hall*.
       Ithaca, N.Y.: Cornell University Press, 1976. Pp. 436.

       Includes re-examinations of major events such as British
       intervention in Malaya in the 1870s and discussion of
       methodological and interpretive problems.

30.   Crawford, Hunter A. "The Birth of the Duff Development
       Company in Kelantan 1900-1912." *Malaysia in History*
       13:3-9.

       Description of the monopolistic tin and rubber enter-
       prise that dominated the state of Kelantan before and
       after the British take-over in 1909. By an employee of
       plantation agencies in Penang.

31.   Crawfurd, John. *A Descriptive Dictionary of the Indian
       Islands and Adjacent Countries*. Kuala Lumpur: Oxford
       University Press, 1971. Pp. 459.

       Encyclopedic work by early member of the Indian medical
       service who later became British resident in Singapore.
       Land, peoples, commerce, biographies. First published in
       1856. See also entry 382.

32.   ———. *History of the Indian Archipelago Containing
       an Account of the Manners, Arts, Languages, Religions,
       Institutions and Commerce of Its Inhabitants*. 3 vols.
       Edinburgh: A. Constable and Company, 1820. See also
       entry 382.

33.   *Cunyngham-Brown, J.S.H. *The Traders: A Story of Britain's
       South-East Asian Commercial Adventure*. London: Newman
       Neame Ltd. for Guthrie and Company, 1971. Pp. 352.

A history of one of the largest trading firms, whose development was coterminous with British rule in the straits. Informative on tin, rubber, agency houses, immigrant labor, relations between government and business.

34. Daly, D.D. "Surveys and Explorations in the Native States of the Malayan Peninsula 1875-1882." *Proceedings of the Royal Geographical Society* 7:393-412.

    Especially instructive on geology in addition to providing the general survey of lands and peoples characteristic of early treatments. By a surveyor and officer of the public works department.

35. *Dennys, N.B. *A Descriptive Dictionary of British Malaya*. London: London and China Telegraph Office, 1894. Pp. 423.

    Ethnographic, linguistic and geographic presentation by an early member of the Chinese Protectorate.

36. *Dew, A.T. "Exploring Expedition from Selama, Perak to Pong, Patani." *SBRAS* 19:105-120.

    Account of a survey made on the orders of the government of Perak to determine the feasibility of making a road connecting British and Siamese territory. Interesting down-to-earth description of land and people.

37. *Dickson, Sir J.F. "Straits Settlements and British Malaya." *English Illustrated Magazine* (Jan. 1890) 283-292.

    General description covering history, government and peoples and including the Borneo territories. By the colonial secretary of the straits settlements.

38. Doyle, Patrick. *Tin Mining in Larut*. London: E. and F.N. Spon, 1879. Pp. 32.

    An informative account, with technical details of the kind that prospective miners and investors would find helpful. Written five years after the British formally assumed responsibility for this part of Perak.

39. Drabble, J.H. "Investments in the Rubber Industry in Malaya c.1900-1922. *Journal of Southeast Asian Studies* 3:247-261.

    Taken from dissertation, University of London. Examines investment patterns of native and foreign growers and the influence of rubber on retail markets not directly related to it.

40.   ————. *Rubber in Malaya 1876–1922.* Kuala Lumpur: Oxford
       University Press, 1973. Pp. 256.

       The definitive monograph on the growth of the industry,
       role of agency houses, relations with government, planter
       associations. Author was employed on a rubber estate and
       later lectured at the University of Malaya.

41.   ————. "Some Thoughts on the Economic Development of
       Malaya Under British Administration." *Journal of South-
       east Asian Studies* 5:199–208.

       Points out that management by government was small
       scale and individualistic, area by area, until the rubber
       boom in the early 1900s. By the 1920s rubber was so impor-
       tant that policy was formed in London, and it is necessary
       to consider Malaya's economy within the frame of reference
       of world developments and not as an isolated case.

42.   Dykes, F.J.B. *Mining in Malaya.* London: Malay States In-
       formation Agency, 1919. Pp. 63.

       A public information booklet based largely on mining in
       the East Pahang and Trengganu regions.

43.   Earl, G.W. *The Eastern Seas, Or Voyages and Adventures in
       the Indian Archipelago in 1832, 1833, 1834, Comprising
       a Tour of Java, Visits to Borneo, the Malay Peninsula,
       etc., Also an Account of the Present State of Singapore.*
       1837. Rpt. London: Oxford University Press, 1971. Pp.
       461.

       Author served as an assistant resident in the straits
       settlements during the 1860s.

44.   Emerson, Rupert. *Representative Government in Southeast
       Asia.* Cambridge: Harvard University Press, 1955. Pp.
       197.

       British government in Malaya is criticized for failing
       to resolve racial differences and for not laying the ground-
       work for democracy. Traces the rise of nationalism.

45.   Esman, Milton J. *Administration and Development in Malaysia*
       Ithaca, N.Y.: Cornell University Press, 1972. Pp. 341.

       A political science study of institution building and
       reform in a plural society.

46.   *Gammans, Sir L.D. *Singapore Sequel.* London: Signpost Press
       1944. Pp. 31.

A booklet in a public information series on the colonies.

47.   ———. *The State of Lukut*. Kuala Lumpur: Huxley Palmer, 1924. Pp. 5.

Reprint of an article on a small district in the coastal area of Negri Sembilan, formerly part of Selangor. History and government.

48.   *Gibson, W.S. *The Laws of the Federated Malay States In Force on December 31, 1934*. 4 vols. London: Roworth, 1935.

General survey and annotation by administrative officer who finished his career as legal adviser to the government of the Federated Malay States.

49.   Graham, W.A. *Kelantan*. Glasgow: Maclehose, 1908. Pp. 139.

A general descriptive work emphasizing land, people, economy and government, written by a British officer serving as adviser to the ruler of Kelantan just before it was turned over to Britain by Siam. Designed as a lure to investors.

50.   Greentree, Richard, and Nicholson, E.W.B., compilers. *Catalogue of Malay Manuscripts Relating to the Malay Language in the Bodleian Library, Oxford*. Oxford: Clarendon Press, 1901.

Greentree served briefly as a cadet in the Federated Malay States in the 1890s.

51.   Gullick, J.M. *Malaya*. London: Ernest Benn, 1963. Pp. 256.

A volume in a series on modern nations. Land, people, history, economy and government. By an officer who joined the Malayan Civil Service in 1945.

52.   ———. *Stories of Early Kuala Lumpur*. Singapore: Donald Moore, 1956. Pp. 100.

Chinese, British and Malays from the 1870s onwards, in the mining area that became the capital of Malaysia.

53.   Hall, D.G. *History of Southeast Asia*. 3d ed. New York: St. Martin's Press, 1968. Pp. 955.

The best-known text, covering the whole of the area from pre-colonial times to the era of nationalism after World War II.

54. *Hughes, T.D. "A Portuguese Account of Johore." *JMBRAS*
     13:111-156.

     Translation of early eighteenth-century journal kept by
     Portuguese officer. Fighting between Portuguese and Dutch.
     Native politics and war.

55. [Hutchinson, G.] London. Royal Commonwealth Society
     Library. "Rubber Planting in Malaya, 1928-1932." Pp. 76.

     Autobiographical account of the recruitment of an assis-
     tant manager of a rubber estate, job training, language
     lessons, the workers on the estate and relations with the
     labor department of the government.

56. Jackson, James C. "Malay Mining Methods in Kinta in 1884."
     Malaysia in History 8:12-18.

     Technical description, with illustrations. By geographer
     Hull University.

57. ———. *Planters and Speculators*. Kuala Lumpur: University
     of Malaya Press, 1968. Pp. 312.

     Monograph on Chinese and European agricultural enter-
     prise in Malaya, 1786-1921.

58. Kaberry, Phyllis Mary. *British Colonial Policy in South-
     east Asia and the Development of Self-Government in
     Malaya*. London: Royal Institute of International Affairs
     1944. Pp. 91.

     Part of an unfinished study on the development of self-
     government in all of the British dependencies in the Far
     East. Deals with policy and administration in the Malay
     states and the straits settlements.

59. Khoo Kay Kim, ed. *The History of Southeast Asia and East
     Asia: Essays and Documents*. New York: Oxford University
     Press, 1977. Pp. 419.

     An attempt to make history a living force in life and
     in national building. Approached from the viewpoint of
     peoples native to the area, as a correction to Eurocentr-
     ity. Incipient nationalism is treated in some detail.

60. ———. *The Western Malay States 1850-1873: The Effect
     of Commercial Development on Malay Politics*. Kuala
     Lumpur: Oxford University Press, 1972. Pp. 244.

Especially useful on the economics of tin mining and
its connections with Chinese social organization, warfare
and British over-rule.

61. Leech, H.W.C. "About Kinta." *SBRAS* 4:21-33.

Account by early British observer in Perak just after
the establishment of British rule. Land, peoples, economy.

62. Lim Chong Yah. *Economic Development of Modern Malaya*.
     Kuala Lumpur: Oxford University Press, 1967. Pp. 388.

A growth study, before and after rubber. British rule,
health and education are seen in the context of the changing economy. Particularly helpful on the relationship
between the government and businesses.

63. Loh Fook Seng. *The Malay States 1877-1895: Political Change
     and Social Policy*. Kuala Lumpur: Oxford University Press,
     1969. Pp. 213.

The political setting from the Perak war to federation.
Society, labor, education, government. Excellent statistics
and tables.

64. Lovat, Lady Alice Mary. *The Life of Sir Frederick Weld,
     GCMG: A Pioneer of Empire*. London: Murray, 1914. Pp.
     427.

A kinswoman's account of a governor of the 1880s. Intimate and informative on the patronage system of appoint-
ment to the colonial service, on men and families, administrative work, relations with native rulers and with
businessmen and on the extent to which governors had a
free hand. Preface by Hugh Clifford, another relative of
the governor, appointed by him to a position in Malaya.

65. *Low, Sir Hugh. *Sarawak, Its Inhabitants and Productions*.
     London: Bentley, 1848. Pp. 416.

Narrative work, land, people, social institutions,
economy, government, slavery. On a little-known Borneo
territory. By the founder of the residency system of
government in British Malaya, who lived in and helped to
govern Sarawak before coming to Malaya in the 1870s.

66. *Macfadyen, Sir Eric. "Twenty-one Years of Rubber." *British
     Malaya* 6:73-75.

Rubber and the world economy. Graphs and statistics. By
an administrative officer who went on to a career in rubber
growing and high level management.

67. McIntyre, W.D. *The Imperial Frontier in the Tropics 1865-1875.* New York: St. Martin's Press, 1967. Pp. 421.

    Based on a University of London dissertation. Discusses formulation of policy and the involvement of other tropical areas in addition to Malaya. Uses British intervention in Malaya as a case in point, showing pragmatism in action.

68. Makepiece, W., Brooke, G.E., and Braddle, R. St. J., eds. *One Hundred Years of Singapore.* 2 vols. London: Murray, 1921.

    Chapters on all aspects of the city's history and life. Those by administrative officers are enlightening on the personality of government and on famous events such as the 1915 mutiny.

69. *Marks, O. "The Association of British Malaya." *British Malaya* 1:31-32.

    Historical sketch of the London-based association of business groups and senior, retired civil servants which lobbied with the British government on Malayan policy.

70. ———. "The Pioneers of Rubber Planting in Malaya." *British Malaya* 1:281-292.

    How the first plants were brought from South America. Major figures in government, science and business.

71. *Maxwell, Sir W. George, and *Gibson, W.S. *Treaties and Engagements Affecting the Malay States and Borneo.* London: James Truscott, 1924. Pp. 205.

    Discussion of the treaties and their relevance in the context of administration. By high-ranking government officer and an officer with both administrative and legal service.

72. *Merewether, Sir E.M. "Outline History of the Dindings from the 17th Century." *SBRAS* 23:35-47.

    A tracing of the history of the enclave on the Perak coast, using Dutch sources from the 1600s onwards and coming down to the British period by means of official reports.

73. *Mills, J.V.G. *The Chronological Table of Straits Settlements Laws.* Singapore: Government Printing Office, 1926.

An up-dating of the original by Sir William Maxwell,
covering the whole period from the 1860s onwards.

74. ————, tr. *Ying-yai Sheng-lan*, by Ma Huan. London: Cam-
    bridge University Press, 1970. Pp. 393.

    Translation with notes and appendices of the classic
    geographical work, "The Over-all Survey of the Ocean's
    Shores," first published in 1433 by Feng Ch'eng-chun.

75. Mills, Lennox A. *British Rule in Eastern Asia*. London:
    Oxford University Press, 1942. Pp. 581.

    Malayan parts are most helpful on the political changes
    that take place from the 1930s forward, especially the
    de-centralization policy of Sir Cecil Clementi. Notes
    that London did not pay much attention to Malaya because
    of its economic success and lack of political upheaval.

76. ————. *Malaya: A Political and Economic Appraisal*.
    Minneapolis: University of Minnesota Press, 1958. Pp.
    234.

    Detailed treatment on the post-1945 period, emphasizing
    the communist insurrection, steps to self-government and
    Malaya's position in the commonwealth of nations.

77. Morrison, Ian. *Malayan Postscript*. London: Faber, 1942.
    Pp. 196.

    A journalistic work by an eye-witness to the fall of
    Malaya. Critical of the Malayan Civil Service for its
    alleged complaisance, which is seen to have contributed
    to the military collapse.

78. Newbold, T.J. *Political and Statistical Account of the
    British Settlements in the Straits of Malacca*. 2 vols.
    Kuala Lumpur: Oxford University Press, 1971.

    By an early member of the straits service who had ad-
    ministrative responsibility before London assumed control.

79. *Norman, Henry. *The Peoples and Politics of the Far East:
    Travels and Studies in the British, French, Spanish
    and Portuguese Colonies, Siberia, China, Japan, Korea,
    Siam and Malaya*. London: Fisher Unwin, 1900. Pp. 608.

80. Pluvier, J.M. *South-East Asia from Colonialism to In-
    dependence*. Kuala Lumpur: Oxford University Press,
    1974. Pp. 571.

A social science overview, usefully detached by contrast with works covering the same period and written by authors with close involvement in events being discussed.

81. *Purcell, Victor. *Malaysia*. London: Thames and Hudson, 1965. Pp. 224.

A survey of the land, people, history, economy and government, with emphasis on the post-1945 period. By a scholar with long administrative experience in Malaya.

82. Robert, Leslie R. "The Duff Syndicate in Kelantan 1900–1902." *JMBRAS* 45: 81–110.

Traces Duff's enterprise and activities from his early career through his negotiations in England and Siam leading to the establishment of his company in Kelantan.

83. Roff, W.R. *Autobiography and Biography in Malay Historical Studies*. Singapore: Institute of Southeast Asian Studies, May 1972.

An occasional paper dealing with the availability of materials such as biographical data in traditional literature, with trends in contemporary scholarship and opportunities for further work.

84. Sadka, Emily. *The Protected Malay States 1874–1895*. Kuala Lumpur: University of Malaya Press, 1968. Pp. 464.

The standard monograph on the period, stressing economy and government in the founding years of the British residency system. Highly informative on the working of interracial administration and the training of Malay members of the service, on mining, education and daily tasks of British officers. For period after 1895, see entry 131.

85. Senftleben, W. *Background to Agricultural Land Policy in Malaysia*. Hamburg: Harrassowitz, 1978. Pp. 347.

A manual of land tenure in relation to administration and economic development.

86. *Sheppard, Mubin. *A Short History of Malaya*. Kuala Lumpur: B.T. Fudge, 1953. Pp. 13.

A brief tracing for readers new to the subject.

87. ———. *A Short History of Negri Sembilan*. Singapore: Eastern Universities Press, 1965. Pp. 114.

Mainly political and genealogical, stressing the difficulties experienced in unifying small units under a para-
mount ruler. Relations with Chinese and British.

88. ————. "A Short History of Trengganu." *JMBRAS* 22:1-74.

Origins of the state from the 1300s onwards. Relations
with neighbors, especially Johore and later Selangor. Uses
Chinese as well as Malay sources. Continues down to World
War II. Valuable appendices on British officers.

89. Sidhu, Jagjit Singh. "Railways in Selangor 1882-1886."
JMBRAS 38:6-22.

An account of the British government's program of
building railways sufficient to the needs of development
without allowing them to come under the control of private
businesses. The roles of F.A. Swettenham and J.P. Rodger
as residents in the critical period.

90. *Skinner, A.M., ed. "A Geography of the Malay Peninsula
and Surrounding Countries." *SBRAS* 1:52-62.

Notes scarcity of maps and work going forward, by
Swettenham, Pickering et al. Usefulness of the work of
administrative officers and their reports.

91. Smith, T.E. "The Cocos-Keeling Islands: A Demographic
Laboratory." *Population Studies* 14:1-37.

Analysis of sixty years of official records including
births, deaths and marriages, in an island group adminis-
tered from Malaya. By a post-1945 officer.

92. Tarling, Nicholas. *Piracy and Politics in the Malay World:
A Study of British Imperialism in Nineteenth Century
South-East Asia*. Melbourne: F.W. Cheshire, 1963. Pp.
273.

British relations with Malay groups in Johore-Riau
during the 1820s and 1830s.

93. *Treacher, Sir W.H. "British North Borneo: Sketches of
Brunai, Sarawak, Labuan and North Borneo." *SBRAS* 12:
13-74.

General description of land, people, government, trade,
history. By an officer who served in Borneo before going
to Malaya where he eventually became resident-general.

94. Tregonning, K.G. "The Early Land Administration and
    Agricultural Development of Penang." *JMBRAS* 39:34-49.

    Covers the period from the 1790s to about 1840, showing
    trends similar to those which developed on the mainland
    of Malaya as the British grappled with systems of land
    tenure and economic development.

95. ————. "The Origin of the Straits Steamship Company
    in 1890." *JMBRAS* 38:274-289.

    Anglo-Chinese cooperation and German competition. Free
    trade and international rivalry in the last years before
    the rubber boom.

96. ————, ed. "Papers on Malayan History." *Journal of South-
    East Asian History*, 1962. Pp. 273.

    Includes "The British Forward Movement in the Malay
    Peninsula 1880-1889" by Eunice Thio.

97. ————. "Penang and the China Trade." *Malaysia in History*
    5:8-12.

    Asserts that the China trade was the compelling reason
    for taking Penang and that strategic considerations were
    less important.

98. Turnbull, C.M. *History of Singapore 1819-1975*. Kuala
    Lumpur: Oxford University Press, 1977. Pp. 384.

    Though it is comprehensive in scope, both topically and
    chronologically, this definitive work provides detailed
    coverage of policy, administration and trade.

99. ————. "The Origins of British Control in the Malay
    States Before Colonial Rule." In J. Bastin and R. Roolvi
    eds. *Malayan and Indonesian Studies*. Oxford: Clarendon,
    1964.

100. ————. *The Straits Settlements 1826-1867: Indian Presi-
    dency to Crown Colony*. London: Athlone, 1972. Pp. 428.

    Especially useful on the imperatives of trade, on
    immigration from China and India and on relations between
    government and business.

101. *Vlieland, C.A. "The Population of the Malay Peninsula."
    Geographical Review, 24:61-78.

Focuses on the major migrations from outside the
country and within Malaya.

102. Wang Gungwu, ed. *Malaysia: A Survey*. New York: Praeger,
1964. Pp. 466.

An overview of history and society with emphasis on
trade, migrations and government.

103. *Weld, Sir Frederick. "The Straits Settlements and
British Malaya." *Proceedings of the Royal Colonial
Institute* 15:266-311.

General descriptive tracing by a governor of the
1880s, presented also as a progress report on economic
development and the growth of administrative stability.

104. Wheatley, Paul. *The Golden Khersonese*. Kuala Lumpur:
University of Malaya Press, 1961. Pp. 388.

Studies in the historical geography of the Malay
Peninsula before the year 1500.

105. Wicks, P.C. "Images of Malaya in the Stories of Sir
Hugh Clifford." *JMBRAS* 52:57-72.

An essay on Clifford's impressions and ideas about
Malayan character and life, taken from a selection of
his prolific writings on the country and its people from
the 1880s to the 1920s.

106. ————, ed. "Journal of a Mission to Pahang, January
15th to April 11, 1887, by Hugh Clifford." *Southeast
Asia Working Paper No. 10*. Honolulu: University of
Hawaii, 1978. Pp. 50.

Describes Clifford's travels as a young officer, sent
by his cousin, the governor, to establish contact with
the ruler of Pahang and arrange for the posting of a
British adviser at his court.

107. ————. "Sir Frank Swettenham and Education in British
Malaya, 1874-1904." *Educational Perspectives* 8:27-32.

The period of Swettenham's rise to the governorship
was also the period of resolving educational policy,
especially with regard to English versus vernacular
curricula and the training of Malays for government service.

108.   *Winstedt, R.O. *Britain and Malaya 1786-1941*. London:
       Longmans Green, 1944. Pp. 79.

       Pamphlet in a series on countries in the commonwealth
       of nations. A brief overview explaining the reasons for
       Britain's intervention in Malaya, her policy and record
       and the economic development of the country in the
       colonial period.

109.   ————. *Malaya and Its History*. London: Hutchinson,
       1962. Pp. 160.

       An extended version of entry 108 carrying the story
       through the reoccupation of the country in 1945, the
       suppression of the communist insurrection and the achieve-
       ment of independence in 1957. See also entry 372.

110.   ————, ed. *Malaya: the Straits Settlements and the
       Federated and Unfederated Malay States*. London: Con-
       stable, 1923. Pp. 283.

       Covers much the same ground, though for a shorter
       period, as is covered in entries 108 and 109. Interesting
       as an indication of official thinking on long-term policy
       and the effectiveness of British rule as of the years
       immediately following World War I.

111.   Wong Lin Ken. *The Malayan Tin Industry to 1914*. Tucson:
       University of Arizona Press, 1965. Pp. 302.

       Expansion after British take-over in 1870s. Rise of
       European enterprise and decline of Chinese control in
       mining. Relationship between private business and govern-
       ment department concerned with welfare of workers.

112.   Wright, A., and Reid, T.H. *The Malay Peninsula*. London:
       T.F. Unwin, 1912. Pp. 360.

       A journalistic collection representing all aspects of
       the country's life. Illuminating on the persona of all
       the government services and the work of the various
       departments.

113.   Wurtzberg, Charles. "History of the Association." *Malaya*
       (Feb. 1952) 25-27.

       Historical tracing of the organization and work of the
       Association of British Malaya in London, from 1867 on-
       wards. The story is completed in a second article, March
       issue, 23-26. See also entry 128.

See also 114, 118, 127, 129, 131, 134, 137, 152, 154, 157,
160, 161, 162, 163, 164, 169, 175, 177, 178, 179, 181,
182, 186, 190, 191, 193, 194, 196, 198, 199, 203, 204,
207, 213, 215, 225, 241, 250, 265, 267, 279, 280, 284,
302, 309, 316, 322, 327, 338, 339, 342, 362, 366, 371,
373, 374, 375, 384, 390, 391, 393, 394, 398, 400, 404,
406, 407, 408, 413, 421, 424, 425, 427, 433, 438, 442,
449, 450, 452, 454, 489, 491, 492, 494.

III. BRITISH POLICY AND ADMINISTRATION

114.   Allen, J. de V. "The Colonial Office and the Malay
        States, 1867-1873." *JMBRAS* 36:1-36.

        Discussion of the thinking in London that led to the
        intervention of 1874 on the mainland. The author makes
        extensive use of official documents.

115.   ————. "The Elephant and the Mousedeer—A New Version:
        Anglo-Kedah Relations 1905-1915." *JMBRAS* 41:54-94.

        Kedah's role in preventing the inclusion of the un-
        federated states in the Federated Malay States in 1909
        when Kedah and three others were taken over from Siam.

116.   ————. "Johore 1901-1914." *JMBRAS* 45:1-28.

        The struggle between the sultan of Johore and the
        British, the former wishing to remain independent and
        the latter aiming at the absorption of the state. Highly
        critical of Sir Frank Swettenham and his personal interest
        in rubber concessions.

117.   ————. "The Kelantan Rising of 1915: Some Thoughts on
        the Concept of Resistance in British Malayan History."
        Journal of South-East Asian History 9:241-257.

        Contends that the rising should be seen as the starting
        point of Malay resistance to the British, culminating in
        the independence movement after 1945.

118.   ————. "Malayan Civil Service, 1874-1941: Colonial
        Bureaucracy-Malayan Elite." *Comparative Studies in
        Society and History* 12:149-178.

        Holds that an understanding of Malaya in the British
        years depends on an appreciation of the power and central
        role of the service, which is described as being repre-
        sentative of elitist thinking in Britain and aloof from
        Malay society. Useful statistics.

119.   ————. *The Malayan Union*. New Haven: Yale University
        Monograph Series (No. 10), 1967. Pp. 181.

        Traces the story of the ill-fated Malayan Union from
        the years before the Japanese invasion forward, using
        interviews with participants and offical documents.

120.   ————. "Two Imperialists." *JMBRAS* 37:41-73.

        Studies of Sir Frank Swettenham and Sir Hugh Clifford,
        drawing on their writings and on official papers and
        relating their personalities and characters to their
        work in Malaya.

121.   *Baker, A.C. "Anglo-Dutch Relations in the East." *SBRAS*
        64:1-68.

        On relations at the start of the nineteenth century,
        especially with reference to Sumatra. Based on records
        in Singapore and Malacca.

122.   Barber, Noel. *A Sinister Twilight*. Boston: Houghton
        Mifflin, 1968. Pp. 364.

        An account of the fall of Singapore in 1942 and the
        background to it. Asserts that a major factor was a
        profound lack of confidence in the civil service on the
        part of the military.

123.   Bassett, D.K. "Anglo-Malay Relations 1786-1795." *JMBRAS*
        38:183-212.

        Points out that even at this early stage the Malay
        rulers were weak and were in close touch with the British
        in Penang, on whom they depended for money and military
        support.

124.   Bastin, John S. *The Development of Raffles' Ideas on the
        Land Rent System in Java and the Work of the Mackenzie
        Land Tenure System*. The Hague: Nijhoff, 1954. Pp. 193.

        Dissertation, Leyden University. Useful in providing
        background information on the important question of land
        tenure systems that were later experimented with in the
        straits settlements and the Malay states.

125.   Beaglehole, J.H. *The District: A Study of Decentralization
        in West Malaysia*. London: Oxford University Press,
        1976. Pp. 122.

A political science approach to the implementation of policy at the local level, focusing on Kelantan. Covers the period from the establishment of British over-rule before 1909 to the 1970s, using annual reports and some personal papers.

126. *Belfield, Sir Henry C. *Handbook of the Federated Malay States*. London: E. Stanford, 1904. Pp. 174.

A public information booklet issued originally by the Emigrants Information Office, for the guidance of potential investors and planters. The author was resident in Selangor at the time of writing.

127. Blakeley, Brian L. *The Colonial Office 1868-1892*. Durham, N.C.: Duke University Press, 1972. Pp. 195.

A study of the formulation of policy and of correspondence with the colonies in the time period when the last great forward movement of Victorian years took place. Especially helpful on the principal actors in the office and their relations with counterparts abroad.

128. *Bryson, H.P. "The Association That Was Born Out of a Colonial Governor's Spending." *Malaysia* (May 1973) 11-13.

Builds on entry 113 and explains the changes that took place in the twentieth century as the association adapted itself to developments in Malaya.

129. Cavenagh, General Sir Orfeur. *Reminiscences of an Indian Official*. London: W.H. Allen, 1884. Pp. 372.

The autobiography of the last governor of the straits settlements under the Indian government before the Colonial Office took control in 1867. Particularly interesting on family backgrounds of officials and the patronage system of recruitment, which continued in effect for the Malay states, and on relations between the government and local groups such as European traders and Chinese businessmen.

130. [*Cavendish, Alexander.] Oxford. Rhodes House Library. IO s.93. "Malaya: Retrospect 1909-1933."

Has special reference to the development of co-operative societies in Malaya, which department was headed by the author.

131.   Chai Hon Chan. *The Development of British Malaya 1896-
       1909*. Kuala Lumpur: Oxford University Press, 1964. Pp.
       366.

       Traces the governmental story from the point where entry
       84 leaves off, continuing to the year when the four north-
       ern states were taken over from Siam. Emphasizes federa-
       tion in 1895, economic development and education. For
       period before 1896 see entry 84.

132.   Chan Su-ming. "Kelantan and Trengganu, 1909-1939." *JMBRAS*
       38:159-198.

       An administrative tracing, based mainly on annual report
       Critical of the British for their interference, while
       maintaining that their continued use of Malay officers
       helped improve local administrations.

133.   Chew, E. "Sir Frank Swettenham and the Federation of
       the Malay States." *Modern Asian Studies* 2:51-69.

       Taken from M.A. thesis, University of Singapore. Critica
       of Swettenham's autocratic approach and the rigid struc-
       ture of the federation as presided over by him.

134.   *Clifford, Sir Hugh. "British and Siamese Malaya." *Pro-
       ceedings of the Royal Colonial Institute* 34:45-75.

       An interesting comparison of the states under British
       control as of 1902 with those to which the Siamese laid
       claim.

135.   ————. *The Further Side of Silence*. New York: Doubleday,
       1927. Pp. 407.

       Maintains that the question of self-government for
       Malaya should be considered in the context of what pre-
       British rule was like in the country. In the author's
       opinion this was cynical, cruel, autocratic and wasteful.
       The British are more benign. But the bringing of modern
       civilization has enchained both the British and the
       Malays.

136.   *Corry, W.C.S. "The Passing of the British Advisers."
       Malaya (Apr. 1957) 22-25.

       A brief look at the system and its development. Examples
       of the greatest of the British officers. Preparation of
       the country for self-government. The work of advisers
       before the war and after.

137. Emerson, Rupert. *Malaysia: A Study in Direct and Indirect Rule*. Kuala Lumpur: University of Malaya Press, 1966. Pp. 536.

    First published in 1937, the book analyzes the structure and functioning of the British system from a political science point of view, using mainly published documents and some interviews. Shorter treatment of Dutch rule in the East Indies. Critical of the British for not being democratic enough.

138. *Gammans, L.D. *Report on Co-operation in India and Europe*. Singapore: Government Printer, 1933. Pp. 314.

    Author spent a year surveying the Indian and European systems. The report reflects his experience outside Malaya and also his work as a co-operatives officer in that country.

139. Great Britain. Colonial Paper 194. *Report on a Mission to Malaya*, by Sir Harold MacMichael. London: HMSO, 1946. Pp. 16.

    Raises the question of whether the Malay rulers had been asked to concede too much of their autonomy in the interests of the Malayan Union plan immediately following the war.

140. Great Britain. Command Paper 1320. *Further Correspondence Relating to the Affairs of Certain Native States in the Malay Peninsula, in the Neighborhood of the Straits Settlements*. London: HMSO, 1875. Pp. 125.

    Contains despatches exchanged between the governor and London and also correspondence on appointments of officers to administrative posts in Perak, Selangor and Sungei Ujong.

141. Great Britain. Command Paper 3235. *Report by the Rt. Hon. W.G.A. Ormsby-Gore on His Visit to Malaya, Ceylon and Java During the Year 1928*. London: HMSO, 1928, Pp. 166.

    Problems of recruitment for the civil services after 1918, conditions of service in the colonies, comparisons with Dutch methods. Critical of examination recruitment and of British education in relation to what is needed in the colonies.

142. Great Britain. Command Paper 4276. *Report of Brigadier-General Sir Samuel Wilson, Permanent Under-Secretary of*

State for the Colonies, on His Visit to Malaya. London: HMSO, 1933. Pp. 46.

Visit undertaken to investigate views of the civil service and public opinion generally in relation to the decentralization policy of the governor. Supports the policy but urges restraint in implementation.

143. Great Britain. Command Paper 6749. *Malayan Union and Singapore: Summary of Proposed Constitutional Arrangemen* London: HMSO, 1946. Pp. 10.

The controversial Malayan Union proposal discussed and its proposals explained.

144. Great Britain. Command Paper 7171. *Federation of Malaya: Summary of Revised Constitutional Proposals*. London: HMSO, 1947. Pp. 20.

Revision of the Malayan Union policy in the light of criticism and opposition among the rulers and others.

145. Great Britain. Federated Malay States. *Correspondence Respecting the Federation of the Protected Malay States, May 1893 to December 1895*. Taiping: Government Printer, 1896. Pp. 29.

Despatches and letters exchanged between London and the governor referring to the system of administration and the attitudes of British and Malays on the question of reform and its legal implications.

146. Great Britain. Federated Malay States and Straits Settlements. *The Malayan Civil List 1940*. Singapore: Government Printer, 1940. Pp. 830.

Complete service records of officers in all branches of the service, together with education and other details. The volume also includes information on retired officers and on posts, salaries and governmental organization. The last such list, all subsequent ones being less informative and detailed.

147. Great Britain. Federated Malay States. *Minutes of the Session of Chiefs of the Federated Malay States Held at Kuala Kangsar, Perak on the 14th, 15th, 16th and 17th July 1897*. Taiping: Perak Government Printing Office, 1897. Pp. 20.

A record of verbal exchanges among British, Malays, Chinese et al., on matters of common concern, mainly political, as the federation gets under way.

148. Great Britain. Federated Malay States. Department of Public Instruction. *Report of the Commission of Inquiry Into the System of English Education in the Colony.* Singapore: Government Printer, 1902. Pp. 87.

    Discusses the pros and cons of English versus vernacular schooling in relation to the administrative and economic needs of the country and the wishes of the people.

149. Great Britain. Federation of Malaya. *The Federation of Malaya and Its Police 1786-1952.* Kuala Lumpur: Grenier, 1952. Pp. 43.

    A short history, together with a description of the country and its people, for use in recruitment of police officers. Part III, on the communist insurrection, is especially informative.

150. Great Britain. Straits Settlements. *Report of the Commissions Appointed by H.E. the Governor of the Straits Settlements and the High Commissioner of the Federated Malay States to Enquire Into Certain Matters Relating to the Public Service.* Singapore: Government Printer, 1919. Pp. 243.

    The Bucknill report on conditions of service and the need for reform. 85 pages of appendices, mainly testimony of civil servants, businessmen and others.

151. Great Britain. *Report of the Committee on the Malayanization of the Government Service.* Kuala Lumpur: Government Press, 1954. Pp. 124.

    An illuminating presentation of the problems of preparing Malays for civil service positions as the country nears independence.

152. *Guillemard, Sir Lawrence. *Trivial Fond Records.* London: Methuen, 1937. Pp. 187.

    Autobiography, mainly administrative, of the years 1919 to 1927 when the author was governor. Also deals briefly with civil service in London before. Helpful on the policy of decentralization, on intra-service rivalries and on racial problems.

153. Gullick, J.M. "Selangor 1876-1882 The Bloomfield Douglas Diary." *JMBRAS* 48:1-51.

    An excellent presentation and annotation dealing with one of the most controversial of the early residents. Calm

and objective on a subject that has been rather lightly
dismissed in the past. By a post-1945 officer with much
local knowledge and high scholarly qualifications.

154.   Hardinge, Sir Arthur. *The Life of Henry Howard Molyneux
        Herbert, Fourth Earl of Carnarvon 1831-1890.* 3 vols.
        London: Oxford University Press, 1925.

        Carnarvon was colonial secretary twice and under-
        secretary once in the period from the 1850s to the 1870s
        when the straits settlements were taken over by the
        Colonial Office and when residents were posted to the
        courts of the west coast rulers. Interesting on the
        cabinet and Whitehall in mid-Victorian times.

155.   *Harrison, C.W. *Some Notes on the Government Services in
        British Malaya.* London: Malayan Information Agency,
        1929. Pp. 152.

        A booklet prepared for use in recruitment, pointing out
        the advantages of a civil service career, the attractions
        of Malaya and the conditions of service such as leaves
        and pensions. An interesting documentation of the changes
        that came to the country from the 1870s to the 1920s.

156.   *Hawkins, Gerald. "The Passing of the MCS." *The Straits
        Times Annual* (1967) 121-126.

        A brief sketch of the great men of the Malayan Civil
        Service, of others less well-known and of the changing
        occupations of the service over the years. Includes Malay
        as well as British officers.

157.   Heussler, Robert. *British Rule in Malaya: The Malayan
        Civil Service and Its Predecessors, 1867-1942.* Westport,
        Conn.: Greenwood Press, 1981. Pp. 356.

        The administrative services of the straits settlements
        and the Malay states from 1867 to 1942. Backgrounds in
        England, education, recruitment, work in Malaya, policy
        and politics.

158.   Jackson, James C. "Batang Padang Ninety Years Ago."
        Malaysia in History 10:31-38.

        A traveller in Perak during the 1870s, noting adminis-
        trative problems, agriculture, mining, race relations.

159.   [*Jervois, Gen. Sir William.] New Haven. Master's Library.
        Berkeley College, Yale University. General Sir William
        Jervois Papers.

Diaries and other papers of a governor of the 1870s, including journal of visits to Malay rulers.

160. *Jones, S.W. *Public Administration in Malaya*. London: Oxford University Press, 1953. Pp. 229.

A definitive work on all aspects of government during the British years, by a distinguished civil servant who rose to be colonial secretary of the straits settlements. Useful on service organization, on the main policy developments, on political issues and on Malayanization and reconstruction after 1945.

161. Khoo Kay Kim. "The Federation of 1896: The Origins." *Peninjau Sejarah* 1:6-23.

A polemical essay on why the federation was made, backed by official records of the time. Contends that the insolvency of Pahang was the key.

162. ———. "The Origin of British Administration in Malaya." *JMBRAS* 39:52-91.

Asks why the British intervened in 1874 on the mainland and holds that the fostering of trade was the prime mover. Deprecates imperial motives of the political and military kind, noting that these had less weight in the Gladstonian era.

163. ———. "The Pangkor Engagement of 1874." *JMBRAS* 47:1-12.

Argues that Pangkor was not a major departure since trade antedated it, as did political interference. Nor was much changed after Pangkor, which is seen as a symbolic more than a practical matter.

164. *Linehan, W. "A History of Pahang." *JMBRAS* 14:1-256.

The standard history, based on oral traditions and local sources together with British records. Especially helpful on the rebellion of the 1890s. Continues to the 1930s.

165. Liston, C.S. *Report on the Administration of the Federated Malay States, 1919*. Rangoon: Government Printer, 1920.

Written by a visiting officer of the Indian Civil Service, the report is interesting for the light it sheds on comparisons between Malay and Indian methods and viewpoints.

166. Loh Fook Seng. "The Beginnings of Higher Education in
        Singapore: Raffles College 1928-1938." *Malaysia in
        History* 9:9-17.

        Winstedt's investigations in the Philippines and Java.
        Sultan Idris Training College in Perak. The initiatives
        of the Methodists in Singapore and financial support from
        the Singapore Chinese community. Literary versus vocational
        instruction, English versus vernacular.

167. ―――――. "Malay Precedence and the Federal Formula in
        the Federated Malay States." *JMBRAS* 45:29-50.

        The record of giving first consideration to the Malays
        over other racial groups, from the Anglo-Siamese treaty
        of 1909 onwards and the background of the federation it-
        self in the 1890s.

168. *Low, Sir Hugh. "The Journal of Sir Hugh Low, Perak,
        1877." Ed. Emily Sadka. *JMBRAS* 28:5-108.

        A diary of the first few months of Low's pioneering
        residency, during which he worked out relationships with
        Malay royals, Chinese community heads and others, and
        put the administration of Malay's premier state on a
        sound basis of public order and finance. Useful annota-
        tions by the editor.

169. *Macfadyen, Sir Eric. "Constitutional Development of
        Malaya." *British Malaya* (Oct. 1943) 214-216.

        The Malayan experience is cited in support of the thesis
        that the empire is strong in its extremities and weak
        at the center.

170. McIntyre, W.D. "Britain's Intervention in Malaya: The
        Origin of Lord Kimberley's Instruction to Sir Andrew
        Clarke in 1873." *Journal of South-East Asian History*
        2:47-69.

        Further speculation on the underlying and immediate
        reasons for intervention and on the question of whether
        or not Clarke was given specific leave to proceed as he
        did.

171. *McNair, J.F.A. *Prisoners Their Own Warders*. London:
        Constable, 1899. Pp. 191.

        A record of the prison at Singapore, maintained for
        Indian convicts, 1825-1873, one of the main uses to which
        India put the straits settlements. Much interesting dis-

cussion of inter-racial society. Written jointly with
W.D. Bayliss.

172.   *Macpherson, Sir John. "Colonialism and the Commonwealth."
       Journal of the Royal Commonwealth Society 3:125-129.

       Parliament takes more interest in the colonies after
       1945 than before, though ignorance of the overseas posses-
       sions remains rife. England knows little about the colo-
       nial service, which is seen as a haven of reaction. De-
       fines the process of devolution and points out its diffi-
       culties.

173.   *Mahmud bin Mat, Dato' Sir. "The Great Flood." *Malaya in
       History* 3:90-95.

       Includes a down-to-earth account of British and Malay
       officers of the Malayan Civil Service working together
       at the district level in the inter-war years.

174.   *Marriott, Sir Hayes. *Straits Settlements Census*. Singa-
       pore: Government Printer, 1911. Pp. 154.

       Land area, dwellings, population, religion, age, sex,
       civil condition, race, language, occupations.

175.   Maxwell, Sir Peter Benson. *Our Malay Conquests*. London:
       P.S. King, 1878. Pp. 124.

       By the recorder of Penang and chief justice of the
       straits settlements. An anti-imperial polemic, suggest-
       ing inter alia that the British were unjust in their
       treatment of the defeated Malays after the Perak war of
       the 1870s. Compare with entry 184.

176.   *Maxwell, Sir W. George. "The Administration of Malaya."
       British Malaya (May 1943) 153-158.

       Maintains that the federation of the 1890s was hurried,
       that the decentralization of the 1930s was ill-considered
       and that the interests of the Malay rulers have been
       honored in the breach throughout.

177.   *Middlebrook, S.M., and Pinnick, A.W. *How Malaya is
       Governed*. London: Longmans, 1949. Pp. 188.

       A general treatment written for civics classes in
       secondary schools. Traces the history of the subject and
       describes the structure and operation of the government
       in all its branches.

178. Mills, Lennox A. *British Malaya 1824-1867*. Kuala Lumpur:
         Oxford University Press, 1966. Pp. 424.

         An excellent survey of policy and government, including
         details of civil service recruitment and work in the peric
         before the Colonial Office assumed control.

179. Milner, A.C. "The Federal Decision: 1895." *JMBRAS* 43:104-
         115.

         Contends that the London end of the story has been
         overdone, as has the Pahang explanation. Calls for more
         work on the activities of men on the spot at the time and
         less emphasis on high policy.

180. Nathan, R.S. "Development of District Administration in
         Batang Padang." *Malaysia in History* 13:20-32.

         Organization of the district from the 1880s forward.
         Economy, justice, communications, police, public works.
         Major actors such as Swettenham. Revenue and land adminis-
         tration. Health and education. Ends in 1900.

181. Nicolson, I.F., and Hughes, Colin A. "A Provenance of
         Proconsuls: British Colonial Governors 1900-1960."
         The Journal of Imperial and Commonwealth History 4:
         77-106.

         Families, schooling, recruitment, characteristics of the
         various positions, changes over time, attitudes and styles

182. Parkinson, C.N. *British Intervention in Malaya 1867-1877*.
         Singapore: University of Malaya Press, 1960. Pp. 384.

         Summation of a number of studies made of various aspects
         of the problem, such as immediate and ultimate causes,
         as viewed in London and on the scene, activities of mer-
         chants, native rulers and Chinese, influences from India.
         Discusses prominent officials and their importance and the
         sensibilities of groups in straits society in the time
         period. Based on official documents.

183. *Pepys, W.E. "Kelantan During World War I." *Malaysia in
         History* 6:36-39.

         Life in Kelantan during the first decade of British
         rule. The outbreak of 1915. The ruling family and British
         officers such as Langham-Carter, George Maxwell and H.W.
         Thomson. Village headmen. Author served in the state durin
         the period.

184. Plunket, C.M. *Enquiry As to Complicity of Chiefs in Perak Outrages: Precis of Evidence and Abridgement of Evidence.* Singapore: Government Printer, 1876.

By an officer closely involved in the disturbances and the aftermath. Discusses evidence, charges, the defense. Usefully read alongside entry 175.

185. [*Purcell, Victor.] London. Royal Commonwealth Society Library. "A Malayan Union." Pp. 24. Typescript.

Written during World War II. Traces the administrative diversity of the country during the British period and suggests the need for unity in meeting the needs of a modern industrial age. Interesting as an example of civil service thinking at a time when planning was going forward with regard to organization of the country after liberation.

186. Satwant, Ahluwalia Singh. "Administration in Ulu Selangor District, West Malaysia." M.A. thesis, University of Singapore, 1970.

A political science thesis with a useful historical introduction discussing officers in the 1880s, the preoccupations of early residents and particular lines of work.

187. Sidhu, Jagjit Singh. "Sir Cecil Clementi and the Kuomintang in Malaya." *Malaysia in History* 9:18-21.

Discussion of the attempt of the governor in the early 1930s to control the subversive activities of the Chinese nationalists in Malaya.

188. Smith, T.E. "The Effect of Recent Constitutional Changes on the Public Service in the Federation of Malaya and Singapore." *Public Administration* 37:267-273.

The effects of independence on the Malayan Civil Service, with special reference to pensions. Includes figures on numbers of administrative and other officers still in service as of the late 1950s. By a post-1945 officer.

189. Stevenson, Rex. *Cultivators and Administrators: British Educational Policy Towards the Malays 1875-1906.* Kuala Lumpur: Oxford University Press, 1975. Pp. 240.

The evolving attitudes of the British on education for Malays, beginning with the first residents on the west

coast, and ending with the founding of the Malay College,
established to train Malays for government service. Especially valuable for its discussion of Wilkinson and the
other major figures and for insights into Malay views at
the time.

190.   *Swettenham, Sir Frank. *British Malaya*. London: Allen and
       Unwin, 1955. Pp. 380.

       A wide ranging descriptive work by an officer who served
       from the 1870s to 1903 and rose to the governorship. Land,
       people, history, government. The classic apologia for
       British rule and, as such, controversial.

191.   ————. "British Rule in Malaya." *Proceedings of the
       Royal Colonial Institute* 27:273-312.

       A description and justification, given as a paper before
       a learned audience. Interesting for the picture it pro-
       vides of official thinking at the time of the federation
       which the author considered his own creation and inspira-
       tion.

192.   Tarling, Nicholas. "Sir Cecil Clementi and the Federation
       of British Borneo." *JMBRAS* 44:1-34.

       Examination of a side issue, much neglected due to the
       attention given by many scholars to Clementi's policy of
       decentralization in the Federated Malay States.

193.   ————. *Imperial Britain in South-East Asia*. Kuala Lumpur:
       Oxford University Press, 1975. Pp. 273.

       A collection of essays on imperial policy and foreign
       relations with regard to Malaya and other British depen-
       dencies in the area.

194.   Thio, Eunice. *British Policy in the Malay Peninsula 1880-
       1910*. 2 vols. Kuala Lumpur: University of Malaya Press,
       1969.

       Extension of political control, the forward policy,
       administrative reorganization, the Pahang problem, federa-
       tion and the tightening hold on Johore.

195.   *Thomas, Sir Shenton. *The Present Position in Malaya*.
       London: Eyre and Spottiswoode, 1936. Pp. 32.

       Over-all appreciation by the last pre-war governor.

196. Tilman, Robert O. *Bureaucratic Transition in Malaya.*
     Durham, N.C.: Duke University Press, 1964. Pp. 175.

     The British tried not to disrupt tradition, but their
     very presence and work had that effect. Malays served in
     the administration from the first. The relatively large
     numbers of them towards the end of the British period
     eased the move to self-rule. Figures on British and Malay
     officers.

197. ─────. "Nationalization of the Colonial Services in
     Malaya." *South Atlantic Quarterly* 61:183-196.

     Replacement of British officers by Malays. The Malayan-
     ization scheme, negotiations in London, effects on effi-
     ciency in Malaya.

198. *Treacher, Sir W.H. "British Malaya, With More Especial
     Reference to the Federated Malay States." *Journal of
     the Society of Arts* 55:493-512.

     A talk given before the colonial section of the society
     in 1907. Swettenham in the chair. Land, people and history.
     Covers Borneo and Burma as well as Malaya.

199. Tregonning, K.G. *The British in Malaya, 1786-1826.* Tucson:
     University of Arizona Press, 1965. Pp. 186.

     Uses straits settlements documents to trace the first
     forty years of British rule, including commercial rela-
     tions with the Malay states. Describes the influence of
     traders who wanted to break the company's monopoly after
     the decline of the China trade.

200. Trevelyan, Sir George. *The Competition Wallah.* New York:
     AMS Press, 1977. Pp. 355.

     Letters written by a member of the Indian Civil Service
     to a friend in England in the 1860s, providing a picture
     of service life and attitudes that bear a striking re-
     semblance to views and conditions in the straits settle-
     ments, then ruled from India.

201. *Vlieland, C.A. *British Malaya.* London: Crown Agents,
     1931. Pp. 389.

     A report on the 1931 census and on problems of gather-
     ing vital statistics.

202.   *Winstedt, R.O. "Decentralization in Malaya." *Asiatic
        Review* 32:602-610.

        A low-key, informative comment on the issue that was
        exercising the senior ranks of the service in the early
        1930s and which eventuated in the recall of the governor.

See also 9, 10, 11, 14, 17, 23, 24, 28, 44, 45, 58, 63, 64,
        67, 71, 75, 84, 85, 87, 88, 100, 109, all entries in Chap-
        ter IV, 291, 292, 302, 304, 310, 320, 322, 323, 338, 339,
        341, 342, 356, 360, 366, 377, 384, 386, 390, 400, 416,
        453, 469, 491, 492, 499.

IV. BIOGRAPHY AND AUTOBIOGRAPHY

203. Abd Allah ibn 'Abd al-Kadir. *The Autobiography of Munshi Abdulla.* Singapore: Methodist Publishing House, 1918. Pp. 146.

A classic testimony by Raffles' scribe, illuminating Malay thinking on close relations between the races in the earliest years. See entry 315.

204. Abdul Majid bin Zainuddin, Haji. *The Wandering Thoughts of a Dying Man.* Ed. W.R. Roff. Kuala Lumpur: Oxford University Press, 1978. Pp. 169.

Memoirs of a teacher in Malay College in the early years of the twentieth century, ending in 1923. Later a pilgrimage officer in Mecca. Excellent on the first years of the college, on major figures such as Wilkinson and on British and Malay attitudes.

205. *Adkins, E.C.S. "Malayan Portraits." *Malaya* (Sept. 1953) 527-529.

Sketches of Pickering and other important figures, by a member of the Chinese Protectorate.

206. Ainsworth, Leopold. *The Confessions of a Planter in Malaya.* London: Witherby, 1933. Pp. 224.

A public school man who arrived in Malaya at eighteen to start as a junior on a Kedah estate. Intimate look at rubber planting in all its manifestations: planters, civil servants, workers, the economy, social life, morale.

207. *Anson, Maj. Gen. Sir Archibald E.H., KCMG. *About Others and Myself.* London: Murray, 1920. Pp. 398.

The first lieutenant governor of Penang under the Colonial Office, 1867. Excellent on the patronage system, family background, life in the straits, government, relations with Malays and Chinese and with the traders.

208.   *Barrett, E.C.G. "Sir Richard Winstedt." *Dictionary of
        National Biography*, in press.

        Sketch of the most prolific scholar-administrator in
        the Malayan Civil Service.

209.   [*Barron, J.M.] Oxford. Rhodes House Library. (M) J.M.
        Barron papers.

        Recollections of a labor department officer, inter-
        war years. Informative on administrative and social life
        in the MCS generally.

210.   [*Barron, W.D.] Oxford. Rhodes House Library. (M) W.D.
        Barron papers.

        Recollections of MCS life and work, in the inter-war
        years mainly, by an officer of the Malay stream.

211.   Bastin, John S. *Sir Thomas Stamford Raffles*. Liverpool:
        Ocean Steamship Company Ltd., 1969. Pp. 22.

        The Raffles-Minto manuscript collection.

212.   [*Birch, Sir E.W.] Oxford. Rhodes House Library. IO s.242
        Sir E.W. Birch papers.

        Memoirs of MCS service from the 1870s to the early
        twentieth century, ending as resident in Perak. Particu-
        larly helpful on day-to-day tasks and on relations among
        the races and occupational groups in the Federated Malay
        States and earlier in the straits settlements.

213.   *Birch, J.W.W. *The Journals of J.W.W. Birch, First British
        Resident to Perak 1874-1875*. Ed. P.L. Burns. Kuala
        Lumpur: Oxford University Press, 1976. Pp. 410.

        Journals cover the years of the residency, including
        travels throughout Perak and many encounters with leading
        chiefs and with others such as Chinese and European busi-
        nessmen. These are preceded by a lengthy and most helpful
        introduction by the editor, drawing on official documents
        and setting the journals in historical context.

214.   [*Blackwell, K.R.] Oxford. Rhodes House Library. IO s.90.
        K.R. Blackwell papers.

        Memoir of the inter-war years by a member of the Malay
        stream of the MCS. Especially useful on relations between
        Malays and Europeans in administrative situations and
        also in such institutions as rotary clubs, which the auth
        helped to found.

215. Boulger, Demetrius Charles de K. *The Life of Sir Stamford Raffles*. London: Marshall, 1899. Pp. 403.

     Biography of the founder of British Singapore in 1819.

216. *Caldecott, Sir Andrew. *Oxford: A Satire*. Oxford: The Holywell Press, 1907. Pp. 16.

     Verses on university life, by a graduate about to embark on a career in the MCS, leading on to the governorships of Hong Kong and Ceylon.

217. *Cator, G.E. "I Remember: A Malayan Cadet in 1907." *British Malaya* (Feb. 1941) 159-161.

     Memories of the cadet contingent of 1907, selection, the voyage out, first postings, language training.

218. ———. "Malayan Portraits: Raja Idris." *Malaya* (Feb. 1954) 89-90.

     On the sultan of Perak, 1887-1916. Personal recollections of a former Perak resident who knew the sultan earlier in his career.

219. ———. "Sir Hugh Low, GCMG." *Malaya* (Aug. 1958) 36-48.

     On the founder of the residency system in Perak, by one of Low's successors in the position of resident. Covers Labuan as well.

220. [*Churchill, W.F.N.] London. Royal Commonwealth Society Library. W.F.N. Churchill papers.

     Vignettes on district officers, on administration, personalities and impressions of Malayan life.

221. *Clifford, Sir Hugh. *Bush-Whacking and Other Asiatic Tales and Memories*. London: Heinemann, 1929. Pp. 331.

     Stories, mainly on Pahang in the 1880s and 1890s. Ambivalent on Europeanization and on Malay virtues. Escorting Malay royals in England.

222. ———. "Concerning Conrad and His Work." *The Empire Review* 47:287-294.

     On Joseph Conrad and the author, their respective views of the East and Europe's role there. Quotes from letters he received from Conrad and discusses their exchanges on literature.

223.   ————. *A Free Lance of Today*. London: Methuen, 1928.
        Pp. 310.

        Adventure stories in a Malayan setting, based on the
        author's early years in Pahang and his return to the
        country as governor in the 1920s. Fictionalized.

224.   ————. *In Days That Are Dead*. New York: Doubleday,
        1926. Pp. 316.

        Pattern similar to that of entry 223. In addition to
        presenting pictures of Malay life and the European in-
        volvement he muses on imperialism and draws on his own
        youthful experiences to illustrate his points about power
        responsibility and the frustrations of authority.

225.   Clodd, H.P. *Malaya's First British Pioneer: The Life of
        Francis Light*. London: Luzac, 1948. Pp. 166.

        Biography of the ship's captain from India who estab-
        lished British rule in Penang during 1786 and who re-
        mained as governor.

226.   [*Coe, T.P.] London. Royal Commonwealth Society Library.
        T.P. Coe papers.

        Recollections of MCS life and work from 1910 through
        the 1930s, by an officer of the Malay stream.

227.   [*Corry, W.C.S.] Oxford. Rhodes House Library. IO s.215.
        W.C.S. Corry papers.

        MCS officer's career, 1923-1953, including the Japanese
        invasion and service after the war as adviser in Pahang.
        Interesting sidelights on rising Malay political figures.

228.   Coupland, Reginald. *Raffles, 1781-1826*. Oxford: Clarendon
        Press, 1926. Pp. 129.

        A brief account of the start of British administration
        in Singapore and the career of its founder.

229.   *Cunyngham-Brown, Sjovald. *Crowded Hour*. London: Murray,
        1975. Pp. 156.

        Autobiography of a labor department officer in the
        inter-war years and afterwards. Musings on the history
        of the MCS, the eras in its development, on race relation
        and imperialism.

230. Cuscaden, W.L. *Brief Biography of W.A. Cuscaden (1853-*
      1936) in Malaya 1883-1913, Retiring as Inspector-General
      of Police, Straits Settlements. London: W.L. Cuscaden,
      1937.

231. Dalton, Clive (pseud.). *Men of Malaya*. London: Eldon Press,
      1942. Pp. 165.

      Biographies of Light, Raffles, Brooke, Clarke, Low and
      Swettenham. By Frederick Stephen Clark.

232. [*Falconer, J.] Oxford. Rhodes House Library. (M) J. Fal-
      coner papers.

      The varied career of an MCS officer in the inter-war
      years, including service on the east coast and accounts
      of his advisership in Johore and his knowledge of secret
      societies. Ended as resident councillor Penang.

233. [*Gilman, E.W.F.] Oxford. Rhodes House Library. IO s.127.
      E.W.F. Gilman papers.

      Recollections of the father of the labor department,
      covering MCS service of three decades ending in the 1930s.

234. *Gilmour, Andrew. *An Eastern Cadet's Anecdotage*. Singapore:
      University Education Press, 1974. Pp. 174.

      Autobiography by an officer of the Malay stream, cover-
      ing the years from the early 1920s to the 1950s. Extremely
      diverse and interesting service, from district administra-
      tion to high office in Singapore, with major financial
      responsibilities.

235. ————. *My Role in the Rehabilitation of Singapore*.
      Singapore: Institute of Southeast Asian Studies,
      Singapore Oral History Pilot Study #2, April 1973. Pp.
      100.

      Secretariat duties in the 1950s and 1960s. Dealings
      with London on financial matters, controls, planning.
      International conferences, social life, commentary on
      people and events.

236. [*Goode, Sir William.] Oxford. Rhodes House Library.
      IO s.255. Sir William Goode papers.

      Transcript of interview, covering three decades be-
      ginning in 1931, By an MCS officer who had service in
      Aden and was governor of Singapore and later of North
      Borneo. Valuable comments on political figures in Malaya
      after 1945 and on the transition to self-government

in both Malaya and Singapore. The author was the first
chief of state in the latter, having been its last governor under British rule.

237.   *Gordon-Hall, W.A. "Malayan Portraits: H.H. Tuanku
       Muhammad, Yang di-Pertuan Besar, Negri Sembilan, 1898–
       1933." *Malaya* (Nov. 1954) 623–625.

       By an MCS officer who was resident in Negri Sembilan
       after the war and had known the ruler when serving there
       during the inter-war years.

238.   Greentree, Richard. *Poems of the Malay Peninsula*. London:
       Philip Wellby, 1901. Pp. 126.

       Based on the author's experiences as a cadet for a short
       period in the 1890s.

239.   Gullick, J.M. "Captain Speedy of Larut." *JMBRAS* 26:5–103.

       The career of the first assistant resident in Perak
       during the 1870s. By a post-1945 officer. Especially
       helpful on the political situation in which the British
       intervened on the mainland in 1874, on the major per-
       sonalities and on race relations.

240.   [————.] Oxford. Rhodes House Library. (M) J.M. Gullick
       papers.

       Memoranda on the author's service in Malaya during and
       after 1945 and especially on his work as secretary to the
       resident commissioner in Negri Sembilan. Covers the full
       range of administrative tasks.

241.   ————, and *Hawkins, G. *Malayan Pioneers*. Singapore:
       Eastern Universities Press, 1958. Pp. 91.

       Brief biographies of some of the giants of the British
       services, together with descriptions of conditions on the
       ground and daily work.

242.   [*Harvey, J.A.] Oxford. Rhodes House Library. (M) J.A.
       Harvey papers.

       Recollections of service inter-war and after 1945.
       Especially useful on Pahang administration, also Kelantan
       Penang, the Cocos Islands and Perak. Ends career as Briti
       adviser in Pahang.

243.   [*Hay, M.C.] Oxford. Rhodes House Library. IO s.45. M.C.
       Hay papers.

Memoir of service in the labor department and general administration in the unfederated states and in such secretariat posts as the controllership of rubber.

244. [*Hayward, M.J.] Oxford. Rhodes House Library. (M) M.J. Hayward papers.

Lengthy essay on European rule in the East, in the context of an MCS career inter-war and after 1945. Especially thoughtful and interesting on inter-racial government and the contributions of the participating civilizations to the resulting hybrid.

245. [*Helps, E.A.P.] Oxford. Rhodes House Library. (M) E.A.P. Helps papers.

Recollections of an MCS career, stressing the antipathy of the home population to imperialism, the social origins of the officers, reasons for good relations with the Malays and the rights and wrongs of bringing an alien culture to the East.

246. Hockin, John. "After They Left Malaya." *British Malaya* 20: 175-176.

What careers were followed by some representative officers after their service in Malaya. Notes, for example, that Stirling worked in France on the science of crime detection.

247. [*Jarrett, N.R.] Oxford. Rhodes House Library. (M) N.R. Jarrett papers.

An MCS officer's memories of recruitment to the service, his training as a labor officer, relations with planters and later his work as British adviser in Trengganu.

248. [*Jordan, A.B.] Oxford. Rhodes House Library. (M) A.B. Jordan papers.

Recollections of a Chinese Protectorate officer, mainly inter-war. Notes the effects of the Chinese revolution of 1911 on Malaya and speaks of secret societies and the passing of the old Chinese leaders in the country.

249. [*Kempe, J.E.] Oxford. Rhodes House Library. IO s.94. J.E. Kempe papers.

Memoirs and diaries of a 1911 cadet of the Malay stream who retired in the 1930s after a career confined almost exclusively to district and state administrative posts.

Much service on the east coast, especially in Trengganu
and Pahang. Eleven volumes of diaries.

250. Keppel, Admiral Sir Henry. *A Sailor's Life Under Four
      Sovereigns*. 3 vols. New York: Macmillan, 1899.

      Much attention to life and service in straits waters
      and in Singapore and other ports. Local society, race
      relations, prominent personalities, government. A usefull
      external view of the civil service.

251. *Keyser, Arthur Louis. *People and Places: A Life in Five
      Continents*. London: Murray, 1922. Pp. 337.

      By a locally appointed administrative officer. Four
      chapters on Malaya in the late nineteenth century.

252. Khoo Kay Kim. "J.W.W. Birch: A Victorian Moralist in
      Perak's Augean Stable?" *Journal of the Historical Socie*
      4:33-47.

      Holds that it is inconsistent for the British to take
      a position of moral superiority in the matter of Malay
      misgovernment in the 1870s since the first resident in
      Perak is known to have got into debt and is alleged to
      have had ulterior motives in freeing young women from
      slavery.

253. *Leaders of Malaya and Who's Who 1958*. Ed. J.V. Morais.
      Kuala Lumpur: The Economy Printers Ltd., 1958.

      Annual publication, beginning in 1956. For the purposes
      of this bibliography the above edition is the most useful.

254. [*Luckham, H.A.L.] Oxford. Rhodes House Library. (M) H.A.
      Luckham papers.

      Notes on the MCS career of an inter-war and post-war
      cadet. Education in England, recruitment, social life in
      Malaya, administrative service, the clerical staff. In-
      teresting comparisons with Africa, where the writer served
      during World War II.

255. [*Macpherson, Sir John.] Oxford. Rhodes House Library. Sir
      John Macpherson papers (restricted).

      Transcript of interview. MCS administrative career,
      1920s and 1930s, continuing on to governor-generalship of
      Nigeria and permanent under-secretaryship, C.O.

256. [*Mahmud bin Mat, Dato' Sir.] Kuala Lumpur. Malaysian National Archives. Dato' Sir Mahmud bin Mat papers.

    Autobiography of boyhood in Pahang, early twentieth century, Malay College, administrative service ending with high office in the MCS including service under the Japanese.

257. Miller, Harry. *Prince and Premier*. London: Harrap, 1959. Pp. 224.

    Biography of Tunku Abdul Rahman, first prime minister of independent Malaya.

258. [*Milverton, Lord.] Oxford. Rhodes House Library. Lord Milverton papers.

    Transcript of interview of Lord Milverton (Sir Arthur Richards). MCS career beginning in early twentieth century, continuing to governorships, including Nigeria.

259. [*Morkill, A.G.] Oxford. Rhodes House Library. IO. s.66. A.G. Morkill papers.

    Recollections and diaries covering MCS service in Kelantan and the Federated Malay States from 1915 to the 1920s. Especially valuable for an intimate picture of daily work in Kelantan in the early years of British over-rule.

260. [*Moubray, G.A. de C. de.] Oxford. Rhodes House Library. IO s.159. G.A. de C. de Moubray papers.

    Memoir of Trengganu in the inter-war years by MCS officer who was British adviser there at the time of the Japanese attack.

261. *Nairn, P.S. *Poems, Letters and Memories of Philip Sidney Nairn*. Edited by E.R. Eddison. London: Privately printed, 1916. Pp. 171.

    An intimate view of Kelantan before the British take-over in 1909, with background description of Oxford in the early years of the twentieth century and some coverage of Negri Sembilan down to 1914.

262. [*Oakeley, R.H.] Oxford. Rhodes House Library. (M) R.H. Oakeley papers.

    Recollections of Chinese Protectorate work in the inter-war years and after, including office duties, magistracy and inspection of immigrants on arrival in the straits settlements.

263. [*Peel, Sir William.] Oxford. Rhodes House Library. IO
      s.208. Sir William Peel papers.

      Memoir of MCS service 1897-1935, ending as chief secre-
      tary, Federated Malay States and going on to governorship
      of Hong Kong. Excellent on labor department and municipal
      government.

264. *Pickering, William Alexander. *Pioneering in Formosa.*
      London: Hurst and Blackett, 1898. Pp. 283.

      Recollections of adventures and work on the China coast
      and Formosa in the mid-nineteenth century, by the first
      head of the Chinese Protectorate in Malaya.

265. Pope-Hennessey, James. *Verandah.* London: Allen and Unwin,
      1964. Pp. 313.

      The career of Sir John Pope-Hennessey, a nineteenth-
      century colonial governor who started in Labuan where
      Hugh Low, his future son-in-law, was serving. A good deal
      of comment on Low, who became British resident in Perak
      and the founder of the residency system in Malaya.

266. *Purcell, Victor. *The Memoirs of a Malayan Official.*
      London: Cassell, 1965. Pp. 373.

      Administrative autobiography of a Chinese Protectorate
      cadet, mainly in the inter-war years. Especially useful
      on recruitment to the service, language study in China
      and daily work in Malaya.

267. Raffles, Lady Sophia. *Memoir of the Life and Public
      Services of Sir Thomas Stamford Raffles.* 2 vols. London:
      J. Duncan, 1835.

      Biography of the founder of British Singapore, by his
      widow.

268. [*Ramsay, A.B.] Oxford. Rhodes House Library. A.B. Ramsay
      papers.

      Recollections of an inter-war MCS officer, also known
      as Cobden-Ramsay, especially in Kemaman, a district of
      Trengganu, and in Alor Gajah on the west coast.

269. Ribblesdale, Lord. *Charles Lister.* London: T. Fisher
      Unwin, 1917. Pp. 253.

      By the brother of the first resident in Negri Sembilan,
      Martin Lister, briefly mentioning him and providing a

picture of the family and their home in England in the nineteenth century.

270. *Scott, Walter Dare. "Peringatan Senang." *British Malaya* 25:77-80.

Discusses family connections in the East and explains why he ended there. Anecdotes of early administrative service, prominent figures in the country and conditions of work. The first of a series of articles, 1950ff., covering service in the 1890s by an officer who finished his career as adviser in Trengganu.

271. *Sheppard, Mubin. *H.H. The Sultan of Pahang, Sir Abu Bakar ibni Almarhum Sultan Abdullah, GCMG.* Singapore: Donald Moore, 1957. Pp. 36.

Biography of the sultan of Pahang, written for the celebration of the ruler's silver jubilee, by an MCS officer who had known and worked with him.

272. ———. *Taman Budiman: The Memoirs of an Unorthodox Civil Servant.* Kuala Lumpur: Heinemann, 1979. Pp. 278.

Administrative autobiography beginning in the 1920s and continuing through the Japanese occupation to the independence of the country and beyond. By an MCS officer who has published extensively in Malay studies and has made his home in Malaysia.

273. ———. *Tun Perak: Malacca's Greatest Bendahara.* Singapore: Longman, 1969. Pp. 118.

Biography of a prominent Malay royal figure, by an MCS scholar-administrator. Written as a novel.

274. *Skinner, A.M. "Memoir of Captain Francis Light." *SBRAS* 28:1-17.

Uses manuscript material in the British Museum and journals of early officers to provide a portrait of the founder of British Penang. Describes Light's dealings with his superiors in India.

275. [*Stark, W.J.K.] London. Royal Commonwealth Society Library. W.J.K. Stark papers.

Memoir of MCS service on the west coast from 1913 to the 1920s, including labor work and district administration.

276.   Stockwell, A.J. "Sir Hugh Clifford's Early Career 1866–
       1903." *JMBRAS* 49:89–112.

       Taken from private papers in the possession of the
       Clifford family. Boyhood and education. Influences on
       choice of career. Assignment to Pahang by his cousin, the
       governor. North Borneo governorship. Illness, considera-
       tion of early abandonment of colonial service career.

277.   Sulaiman, Sultan of Selangor. "Royal Recollections."
       Malaysia in History 2:16–20.

       By the grandson of the first sultan in the British
       period. Raffles school. Conditions in Selangor during the
       late nineteenth century. Valuable for the picture pro-
       vided of Malay-British relations and for comments on the
       comparative advantages and disadvantages of the two
       cultures.

278.   *Swettenham, Sir Frank. *Also and Perhaps*. London: John
       Lane, 1912. Pp. 303.

       Philosophy of life, musings on human nature and on
       death. Stories of Malaya, including social life and sports

279.   ———. *Footprints in Malaya*. London: Hutchinson, 1942.
       Pp. 176.

       Autobiography of the greatest figure in the civil ser-
       vice of British Malaya, beginning with family and boyhood
       and continuing through his career in Malaya from the 1870s
       to the early 1900s.

280.   ———. *Sir Frank Swettenham's Malayan Journals 1874–
       1876*. Ed. P.L. Burns and C.D. Cowan. Kuala Lumpur:
       Oxford University Press, 1975. Pp. 347.

       Concerned mainly with the author's service as a young
       cadet and focusing on the murder of the resident in Perak
       and the subsequent war.

281.   *Tickell, G.T. "Early Days in Kuala Kangsar." *British
       Malaya* 2:67–70.

       Memories of a local appointee in the late nineteenth
       century in Perak and Selangor. The first of three articles

282.   [Tunku Abdul Rahman.] Oxford. Rhodes Island Library. IO
       s.232. Tunku Abdul Rahman papers.

Transcript of an interview covering the career of a
member of the Kedah aristocracy who became the first prime
minister of independent Malaya.

283.   [*Turner, H.G.] Oxford. Rhodes House Library. (M) H.G.
       Turner papers.

Autobiography of MCS service in the inter-war years and
after, including district administration and much secretariat work in Singapore. First-hand account of the sur-
render of Singapore and brief service under the Japanese,
followed by life in prison camp.

284.   Vetch, Col. R.H., ed. *Life of Lt. Gen. the Hon. Sir
       Andrew Clarke GCMG.* New York: Dutton, 1905. Pp. 353.

Family and career of the second governor of the straits
settlements under the Colonial Office, sent in 1873 to
resolve the difficulties incident to disturbances among
Chinese communities in Perak. Presided over the making of
the Pangkor settlement in 1874 that inaugurated British
rule on the mainland.

285.   [*Weisberg, H.] Oxford. Rhodes House Library. (M) H.
       Weisberg papers.

Recollections of inter-war MCS officer. Especially
informative in the area of public finance.

286.   [*Whitton, C.H.] Oxford. Rhodes House Library. (M) C.H.
       Whitton papers.

Recollections of an inter-war MCS officer who had a
varied career in district and secretariat positions and
who later transferred to the colonial legal service.

287.   *Winstedt, Sir Richard. "Sir Frank Swettenham." *Dictionary
       of National Biography 1941-1950.* London: Oxford Univer-
       sity Press, 1959. Pp. 855-857.

Informative, if somewhat jaundiced, sketch by the most
prolific scholar of the MCS on the most distinguished
administrator in that corps.

288.   ————. *Start from Alif: Count from One.* Kuala Lumpur:
       Oxford University Press, 1969. Pp. 186.

Posthumous autobiographical fragment covering the early
years of the author's MCS career. Most interesting and
helpful on questions of the meeting of East and West,
on inter-cultural exchange and on the extent to which he
thinks understanding is possible or not.

289.   ———.   "R.J. Wilkinson." *JMBRAS* 20:143-144.

    Obituary on the officer who had perhaps the most impressive combination of achievements in administration, educational innovation and scholarship in all of the MCS. Maintains that Wilkinson, who became governor of Sierra Leone, always regretted leaving Malaya.

See also 26, 54, 55, 64, 66, 83, 106, 120, 129, 130, 133, 152, 153, 154, 159, 168, 234, 235, 289, 292, 311, 335, 344, 388, 390, 397, 399, 412, 423, 430, 435, 441, 448, 451, 467, 468, 479, 481, 483, 484, 491, 492, 494, 495.

V. MALAY STUDIES
Including Studies of Malays, Indonesians
in Malaya and Aboriginal Peoples

290. *Adams, T.S. "A Vocabulary of Pangan." *SBRAS* 85:97-123.

291. Allen, J. de V. "The Ancien Regime in Trengganu 1909-
1919." *JMBRAS* 41:23-53.

Holds that Trengganu's government before the British
took over was in many ways better than the Anglo-Malay
regime of 1918, which he portrays in detail, using ar-
chival materials.

292. ————. "Sultan Zainal Abidin III." *Malaysia in History*
12:3-15.

A study of the ruler of Trengganu 1881-1918, based on
the reports of early British officials. The sultan's role
in keeping the British at bay; efficiency of the regime
compared to that of Selangor.

293. *Blackwell, K.R. *Bazaar Malay*. London: Hirschfield Brothers,
1945. Pp. 61.

294. *Blellock, I.W., and *Bryson, H.P. "Ceremonial Custom in
Negri Sembilan." *JMBRAS* 14:272-279.

Record of the full ceremonial followed at the death
and funeral of the ruler and the proclamation of the
accession of his son, in 1933.

295. *Brown, C.C. *Cherita Bualan*. Singapore: Malaya Publishing
House, 1948. Pp. 63.

Literally "a chatty story." Written in Malay, by an
MCS officer with long experience of administration on
the east coast.

296. ————. "Kelantan Bullfighting." *JMBRAS* 6:74-83.

Relates the sport to Malay interests more broadly, notes the history of bullfighting and its origins in Siam.

297. ————. *Malay Sayangs*. London: Routledge, 1951. Pp. 274.

Proverbs, with annotations. Points out that Clifford and Swettenham compared Malay to French, a diplomatic language suited to concealment of meaning and to both courtesy and rudeness. Its subtlety discussed.

298. ————. *Perak Malay*. Calcutta: Federated Malay States Malay Studies Committee, 1921. Pp. 106.

A dictionary in a series of volumes on Malay subjects.

299. ————. *Studies in Country Malay*. London: Luzac, 1956. Pp. 259.

A reader for the study and teaching of the Malay language. Chrestomathies.

300. *Bryson, H.P. "Trengganu Royal Family." *JMBRAS* 11:253.

An explanatory note on a reference to the subject by Winstedt.

301. *Clifford, Sir Hugh. *In a Corner of Asia*. London: T. Fisher Unwin, 1925. Pp. 252.

Social life and customs, tales and impressions gathered during service in the late nineteenth century, principally in Pahang.

302. ————. *In Court and Kampong*. London: The Richards Press, 1927. Pp. 255.

Descriptions of Malay societies and comments on race relations. Holds that Europe neither knows about the East nor cares. The barbarous effects of up-country life on Europeans who serve there.

303. ————. "Life in the Malay Peninsula as It Was and Is." *Proceedings of the Royal Colonial Institute* 30:368-401.

Malay society and ruling classes. Warfare and slavery. Cruelty of the system. Comments, mainly critical, by Sir Hugh Low and Sir Cecil Clementi Smith, who were present.

304. ————. *Malay Monochromes*. London: Murray, 1933. Pp. 312.

Stories of Malay life, social organization and the functioning of government, based on actual experience such

as Low's handling of superstition, and debt slavery in
Pekan. Musings on the effects of British over-rule.

305.   ————. "Some Notes on the Sakai Dialects of the Malay
Peninsula." *SBRAS* 24:13-29.

Social notes on the Sakai aborigines as well as lin-
guistic details and comparisons with Malay.

306.   ————, and *Swettenham, Sir Frank. *A Dictionary of the
Malay Language*. Taiping: Government Printing Office,
1902. Pp. 509.

307.   *Coope, A.E. *A Guide to Malay Conversation*. Singapore:
Kelly and Walsh, 1946. Pp. 67.

A conversation and phrase book, by the author of dic-
tionaries, grammars and readers.

308.   *Dennys, N.B. *Handbook of Malay Coloquial*. London: Trub-
ner, 1878. Pp. 204.

Introductory lessons written for use by business firms
and others. Conversation and phrases.

309.   Gullick, J.M. *Indigenous Political Systems of Western
Malaya*. London: Athlone Press, 1958. Pp. 151.

The definite anthropological study of Malay society and
government, written as a thesis at the University of
London, by a post-1945 officer. Contains historical information and useful comments on inter-racial functioning
with particular reference to cooperation between Malays
and British.

310.   ————. "The Malay Administrator." *Merdeka Outlook*
(1957) 69-83.

Highly informative tracing of Malay participation in
British government from the earliest years of the colonial
period. The Malay feudal base. The continuing role of
traditionalism blended with alien concepts and techniques.

311.   *Hale, A. *The Adventures of John Smith in Malaya 1600-
1605*. Leyden: E.J. Brill, 1909. Pp. 335.

Narrative of a visit to Patani, giving details of Malay
life and government that show remarkable similarity with
conditions encountered by the British three centuries
later. John Smith is a pseudonym for the illegitimate son
of a clergyman and an actress in seventeenth-century
England.

312.   ————. "Folk-Lore and the Menangkaban Code in the
       Negri Sembilan." *SBRAS* 31:43-61.

       Building on the work of Lister the author traces the
       origins of customs and explains their rationale in rela-
       tion to social and political organization.

313.   ————. *List of Malay Proper Names*. Kuala Lumpur:
       Government Press, 1925. Pp. 20.

       Contains a criticism by Clifford.

314.   *Hervey, D.F.A. "Rembau." *SBRAS* 13:241-258.

       Origins of the state, a part of Negri Sembilan, the
       ruling class, geography, population, government and agri-
       culture. By the first straits settlements cadet.

315.   Hill, A.H. "The Hikayat Abdullah: An Annotated Transla-
       tion." *JMBRAS* 28:5-345.

       See entry 203. Annotations useful on the political
       background.

316.   Husin, Ali S. *Malay Peasant Society and Leadership*. Kuala
       Lumpur: Oxford University Press, 1975. Pp. 192.

       A dissertation, University of London. Most enlightening
       on rural conditions and community headships.

317.   *Linehan, W. "The Bendaharas of Pahang." *JMBRAS* 4:334-338.

       Genealogy and something on the character of the rulers,
       their families, relations with society, including Chinese.

318.   *Lister, Martin. "The Negri Sembilan: Their Origin and
       Constitution." *SBRAS* 19:35-53.

       Oral traditions, customs, government. By the first
       resident of the newly organized state.

319.   *Low, Sir Hugh. "Selesilah of the Rajas of Brunei."
       SBRAS 5:1-22.

       A genealogy, literally "book of the descent" of the
       royal family. By an officer who had served for many years
       in neighboring Labuan.

320.   M. "Raja Kamaralzaman ibni Raja Mansur, Raja di-Hilar
       of Perak, the Smiling Civil Servant." *Malaysia in
       History* 8:36-38.

Sketch of sultan Abdullah's grandson, who entered the service in 1918. Illustrates the career of a member of a royal family, educated at Malay College.

321. *McKerron, P.A.B. "A Trengganu Vocabulary." *JMBRAS* 9: 123-128.

322. *McNair, J.F. *Perak and the Malays*. Kuala Lumpur: Oxford University Press, 1972. Pp. 454.

Society, history and government, first published in 1878, by an officer who served in the straits and in the Malay states. Informative on relations between the Malays and the British.

323. *Mahmud bin Mat. "The Passing of Slavery in East Pahang." *The Malayan Historical Journal* 1:8-10.

Defines the institution, explains how it operated in traditional Malay society and what the British did about abolishing it.

324. ————. "Some Features of Malay Life in East Pahang at the Close of the Nineteenth and the Beginning of the Twentieth Centuries." *Malaysia* (May 1964) 20-24.

Feudalism, slavery, festivals, agriculture and village life.

325. *Maxwell, C.N. *The Malay Language and How to Learn It*. Kuala Lumpur: Kyle and Palmer, 1933. Pp. 94.

By a member of the best known civil service family in Malaya. Born in the country.

326. *Maxwell, W.E. "The Folk-Lore of the Malays." *SBRAS* 7:11-29.

Includes religion, housing, diet, weather, birds and animals.

327. ————. "The History of Perak from Native Sources." *SBRAS* 9:85-108.

Based on translation of Malay documents in the author's possession such as books of descent. Covers genealogy and wars. Continued in December 1884 issue.

328. ————. "Malay Proverbs." *SBRAS* 2:85-98.

Uses proverbs to illustrate national character, e.g., "the wisdom of many: the wit of one."

329. ————. *A Manual of the Malay Language.* London: Kegan
      Paul, 1911. Pp. 182.

330. *Maxwell, Sir W. George. *In Malay Forests.* London: Black-
      wood, 1907. Pp. 313.

      Six articles from *Blackwood's Magazine* and others.
      Some tales. Also animals, fish and sport.

331. Morgan, G.T.M. de M. "Brass and White Metal Work in
      Trengganu." *JMBRAS* 24:114–119.

      By a post–1945 officer.

332. *Moubray, G.A. de C. de. *Matriarchy in the Malay Peninsula.*
      London: Routledge, 1931. Pp. 292.

333. *Parr, C.W.C., and *Mackray, W.H. "Rembau, One of the
      Nine States, Its History, Constitution and Customs."
      SBRAS 56:1–77.

      Begins in the fourteenth century. Uses published sources
      and oral history. Both authors served in Negri Sembilan.
      See also entry 359.

334. *Pepys, W.E. "A Kelantan Glossary." *SBRAS* 74:303–321.

      The first published collection of phrases and idioms,
      together with a note on pronunciation.

335. Raja Haji Kamarulzaman. "Some Early Impressions at College
      1905–1908." *Malay College Magazine* 2:58–64.

      Describes the primitive conditions and hard work that
      characterized the college, founded to educate Malays for
      government careers. Speaks with affection of Hargreaves,
      the headmaster, and staff, and of the British officers
      posted to Kuala Kangsar who played games with the students.

336. *Ramsay, A.B. "Indonesians in Malaya." *JMBRAS* 29:119–124.

      Who came, to which parts of the country, and to engage
      in what kinds of work. Compares the Javanese and Malays
      and also the methods of the Dutch and the British.

337. Robert, S.T. "The Trengganu Ruling Class in the Late
      Nineteenth Century." *JMBRAS* 50:25–47.

      A study of the court and Malay administrative officers
      in the years before the British took over, the continuation
      of a measure of self-rule afterwards and the adjustments
      made by both sides.

338. Roff, William R., ed. *Kelantan: Society and Politics in a Malay State*. Kuala Lumpur: Oxford University Press, 1974. Pp. 371.

Collection of papers on various aspects of the subject, including government, religion, social organization and economy. Particularly useful on relations between the British and the Malays in the circumstances of continued Malay responsibility that set the unfederated states off from the federated ones.

339. ———. *The Origins of Malay Nationalism*. Kuala Lumpur: University of Malaya Press, 1967. Pp. 297.

The initial impact of British rule, urbanization, Malay participation in government, education of Malays for administrative and other service, the rise of Malay self-consciousness and the evolution of elites. A valuable, ground-breaking work, indispensable to the subject.

340. Ryan, N.J. "The Malay College 1905-1963." *Malaysia in History* 8:26-31.

Government policy, enrollment, curriculum and student life at the Eton of Malaya. Interesting sketches of Hargreaves, the first headmaster, and of Wilkinson and Sultan Idris.

341. Schricke, Bertram J.O., ed. *The Effects of Western Influence on Native Civilizations in the Malay Archipelago*. Batavia: Kolff, 1928. Pp. 247.

Social studies of a subject that had not yet attracted much attention in the West; made before the rise of nationalism as an influence on scholarship.

342. Scott, James C. *Political Ideology in Malaysia: Reality and the Beliefs of an Elite*. New Haven: Yale University Press, 1968. Pp. 302.

A political science approach, which finds that the mythology of the MCS lives on in the minds of Malaysia's present-day rulers, who have been influenced more by administrative environment than by their own social backgrounds.

343. Seri Lela Di-Raja, Dato'. "The Ulu Trengganu Disturbance May 1928." *Malaysia in History* 12:20-26.

The social background of the uprising, the response of the sultan and his administration, attitudes of the people

and the police, the trial of the rebels and the acts of
the state council.

344.   *Sheppard, Mubin. *The Adventures of Hang Tuah*. Singapore:
       Donald Moore, 1955. Pp. 134.

       A fifteenth-century tale, written by a noted scholar-
       administrator while in a Japanese prison camp during World
       War II.

345.   ————. *Living Crafts of Malaysia*. Kuala Lumpur: Mobil
       Oil Malaysia, 1978. Pp. 118.

       Wood carving, iron smithing, pottery, bead work, screw
       pine mats, kites and bird cage traps.

346.   ————. *The Magic Kite and Other Stories from the Ma'yong*
       Kuala Lumpur: Federal Publications, 1960. Pp. 50.

       Malay folk drama and literature.

347.   ————. *Malay Courtesy*. Singapore: Donald Moore for
       Eastern Universities Press, 1965. Pp. 41.

       A narrative account of manners and customs in everyday
       use.

348.   ————. *The Malay Regiment 1933-1947*. Kuala Lumpur: De-
       partment of Public Relations, Government of Malaya,
       1947. Pp. 52.

349.   ————. *Taman Indera: A Royal Pleasure Ground, Malay
       Decorative Arts and Pastimes*. Kuala Lumpur: Oxford
       University Press, 1972. Pp. 207.

350.   Skeat, Walter W. *Malay Magic*. London: Macmillan, 1900.
       Pp. 685.

       Folk-lore, magic and popular religion. Interesting
       sidelights on communities attributing magic powers to
       early British officers.

351.   ————, and *Blagden, C.O. *Pagan Races of the Malay
       Peninsula*. 2 vols. London: Macmillan, 1906.

       Studies of the Sakai and other aboriginal and non-
       Malay peoples.

352.   *Swettenham, F.A. *About Perak*. Singapore: Straits Times
       Press, 1893. Pp. 78.

Articles reprinted from the *Straits Times* and dealing
with Malay society and government at the time when the
author was resident in Perak.

353. ————. *Malay Sketches*. New York: Lane, 1913. Pp. 288.

Aspects of Malay life, including social customs and
explanations of notorious but little understood subjects
such as "amok."

354. ————. "On the Native Races of the Straits Settlements
and the Malay States." *Journal of the Anthropological
Institute* 16:221-229.

Demographic figures by racial group. Social life and
customs. Trade and government. Author translates a description of the Perak regalia given by Raja Idris, a future
sultan, who accompanied him to the meeting at which this
paper is presented.

355. ————. *The Real Malay*. London: Lane, 1900. Pp. 295.

The Malay race, its ideas, characteristics and culture.
A work widely considered to be the author's definitive
statement on the subject.

356. ————. "Some Account of the Independent Native States
of the Malay Peninsula." *SBRAS* 6:161-202.

The background to the British forward moves in the
mid-1870s. Position of rulers. Internal Perak troubles.
The Larut war. Prominent British officers and their activities, mainly on the west coast.

357. ————. *Stories and Sketches*. Ed. W.R. Roff. Kuala Lumpur:
Oxford University Press, 1967. Pp. 216.

Clans, feudalism, government, slavery. Malay relations
with westerners and vice versa. European influence on
processes of change.

358. ————. *Vocabulary of the English and Malay Languages*.
2 vols. London: W.B. Whittingham and Company, 1881.

359. *Taylor, E.N. "The Customary Law of Rembau." *JMBRAS* 7:
1-30.

Builds on entry 333, adding to the legal details. By
an MCS officer who later transferred to the colonial
legal service.

360. Tilman, Robert O. "The Malay Administrative Service."
      Indian Journal of Public Administration 7:145-157.

      The origins of the plan to provide junior positions
      for Malays, many of whom went on to careers in the MCS.

361. *Wilkinson, R.J. *Events Prior to British Ascendancy.*
      Kuala Lumpur: Government Press, 1924. Pp. 94.

      Notes on the history of Perak before the British for-
      ward move of the 1870s.

362. ———. *A History of the Peninsular Malays.* Singapore:
      Kelly and Walsh, 1923. Pp. 159.

      General tracing. History, social organization, govern-
      ment.

363. ———. *The Incidents of Malay Life.* Singapore: Kelly
      and Walsh, 1920. Pp. 71.

      Malay life and customs, attitudes and folkways.

364. ———. *Malay Beliefs.* London: Luzac, 1906. Pp. 81.

      Religion, magic, superstition.

365. ———. *A Malay-English Dictionary.* London: Macmillan,
      1955. Pp. 631.

      Revision of the original issued in 1903.

366. ———. *Papers on Malay Subjects.* Kuala Lumpur: Oxford
      University Press, 1971. Pp. 468.

      A collection of works on aspects of Malay history,
      society and government and on British over-rule. The
      authors include *Wilkinson, *Winstedt, *Caldecott,
      *Harrison, *Nathan and *Rigby.

367. ———. "Some Malay Studies." *JMBRAS* 10:67-137.

      Beginnings of the Malays in the peninsula, customs,
      dress, political institutions, sorcery, mysticism, the
      Alexander legend in Malaya.

368. ———. *A Vocabulary of Central Sakai.* Kuala Lumpur:
      J. Brown, 1915. Pp. 63.

      Dialect of the Gopeng Valley area.

369. *Winstedt, R.O. "A History of Selangor." *JMBRAS* 12:1-34.

    Mainly genealogy and political history. Taken from
    Dutch sources, government files, earlier histories and
    some Arabic sources.

370. ———. *An English-Malay Dictionary*. London: Paul, Trench
    and Trubner, 1949. Pp. 524.

371. ———. "The Nine States." *JMBRAS* 12:41-114.

    From the fourteenth century to British intervention.
    Lengthy treatment of social and political organization.
    Taken largely from official records and secondary sources.

372. ———. "Notes on the History of Kedah." *JMBRAS* 14:155-
    189.

    Notes towards the fuller treatment in entry 109. Thir-
    teenth to nineteenth centuries, taken from archeological
    evidence, government records and a genealogy provided by
    the British adviser in Kedah.

373. ———, and *Wilkinson, R.J. "A History of Perak." *JMBRAS*
    12:1-180.

    From the sixteenth century to the Perak war, using
    Portuguese documents and British sources. Genealogy, his-
    tory, government, war.

See also 9, 10, 12, 14, 15, 22, 28, 31, 32, 34, 35, 47, 49, 50,
    54, 59, 60, 61, 65, 84, 87, 88, 92, 93, 96, 101, 105, 107,
    109, 115, 116, 117, 123, 131, 132, 135, 145, 153, 158, 164,
    167, 168, 180, 183, 184, 186, 189, 196, 197, 203, 204, 213,
    214, 218, 221, 224, 237, 242, 256, 257, 271, 273, 277, 282,
    394, 408, 421, 423, 440, 461, 467, 469, 475, 476, 478, 482,
    492, 497.

VI. IMMIGRANT PEOPLES: CHINESE AND INDIAN

374. Alexander, G. *Silent Invasion: The Chinese in Southeast Asia*. London: Macdonald, 1973. Pp. 274.

Over-all treatment of Chinese emigration, involving many other countries in addition to Malaya. The parts of China they came from, conditions explaining their departure, lands to which they went, life in the countries of adoption.

375. Arasaratnam, S. *Indians in Malaysia and Singapore*. Kuala Lumpur: Oxford University Press, 1970. Pp. 214.

Historical tracing from the time of early Indian traders and settlers to the last decades of the nineteenth century when the largest numbers came as a result of the rubber boom. Agricultural estates, public works, rubber. Figures and tables by time periods. Life and work. Unionization.

376. *Blythe, W. "Historical Sketch of Chinese Labour in Malaya." *JMBRAS* 20:64-114.

From the fifteenth century onwards. Tin mining, trade, agriculture, rubber. Systems of recruitment in China. Legislation in Malaya. History of the Chinese Protectorate within the MCS.

377. ————. *The Impact of Chinese Secret Societies in Malaya*. London: Oxford University Press, 1969. Pp. 566.

Detailed historical treatment of the societies and the communities within which they grew and functioned, the changing methods of the British in dealing with them, their role in immigration and in the economy. Relations with Malays and others.

378. Comber, L.F. *Chinese Secret Societies in Malaya*. Locust Valley, N.Y.: J.J. Augustin, 1959. Pp. 324.

Mainly the triad societies from 1800 to 1900. Covers Singapore and Penang, the western Malay states and such prominent figures as Yap and Pickering. By a British police officer.

379. *Coope, A.E. "The Kangchu System in Johore." *JMBRAS* 14: 247-263.

Kangchus headed communities of Chinese pioneers which the sultan allowed to form settlements for the purpose of farming and clearing the jungle. From the nineteenth century forward.

380. [Dixon, Alec.] London. Royal Commonwealth Society Library. Alec Dixon papers.

Paper, by a former police officer, on the Chinese Protectorate, its organization and methods in dealing with magistracy, registration of societies, brothels and lodging houses and with control of immigration. Cooperation with police.

381. ————. *Singapore Patrol*. London: Harrap, 1935. Pp. 269.

Police work, mainly among the Chinese. Description of Singapore society. Travel. By a former police officer.

382. *Douglas, F.W. "Malay Place Names of Hindu Origin." *JMBRAS* 16:150-152.

Mainly Selangor, Perak and Johore. Draws on entries 31 and 32.

383. *Fletcher-Cooke, Sir John. "How to Make a Fortune Chinese Style." *Blackwood's* 310:511-524.

Fictionalized account of the experiences of a young MCS officer, newly arrived and assigned legal duties, and his entrapment in the mesh of Chinese society and finance.

384. Gamba, Charles. *The Origins of Trade Unionism in Malaya: A Study in Colonial Labour Unrest*. Singapore: Donald Moore for Eastern Universities Press, 1962. Pp. 511.

Traces the history of the Chinese hongs in the nineteenth century and the gradual unionization of Indian labor in the twentieth. Longer section on the growth of unions and the government's dealings with them from the 1930s onwards. Also covers civil service unions, mainly of clerical workers.

385. *Gammans, L.D. *Co-operation Amongst Indian Estate Labourers.*
     Kuala Lumpur: Kyle and Palmer, 1929. Pp. 12.

     The cooperative societies and their role within estate
     labor communities. By an MCS officer who spent several
     years on special duty with the societies.

386. *Gilman, E.W.F. *Labour in British Malaya.* Singapore:
     Fraser and Neave, 1923. Pp. 44.

     Indian immigration and work on the estates. The activi-
     ties of the Labor Department within the MCS. By the
     father of the department.

387. *Hare, G.T. "The Game of Chop-Ji-Ki." *SBRAS* 31:63-71.

     Gambling in Chinese communities in Malaya. Origins of
     the games in China, their importance to the Chinese and
     methods of hoodwinking the British police.

388. Harrison, C.R. "The Last of the Creepers, Memoirs of a
     Malayan Rubber Planter 1907-1917." *Malaysia in History*
     7:18-27.

     Recollections of a young recruit for work on a rubber
     estate. The system of management, the Indian workers,
     health problems, control of abuses, relations with the
     MCS.

389. Jackson, R.N. *Immigration, Labour and the Development of
     Malaya 1786-1920.* Kuala Lumpur: Government Printer,
     1961.

     The role of Chinese and Indian labor in the Malayan
     economy. By a post-1945 officer in the Chinese Protec-
     torate of the MCS.

390. ————. *Pickering: Protector of Chinese.* Kuala Lumpur:
     Oxford University Press, 1965. Pp. 127.

     Biography of the founder of the Chinese Protectorate
     with emphasis on his years in Malaya and his work with
     the Chinese communities there.

391. Jain, R.K. *South Indians on the Plantation Frontier in
     Malaya.* New Haven: Yale University Press, 1970, Pp. 460.

     The fullest and most detailed treatment of the subject,
     focusing on a Negri Sembilan estate. Tables and statistics.
     Race relations. Rise of trade unions.

392. *Jordan, A.B. *Monthly Review of Chinese Affairs*. Kuala
      Lumpur: Government Printer, 1937. Pp. 52.

      Official report (annual) by the secretary for Chinese
      affairs, Federated Malay States. Covers the political
      situation in China, the role of Chinese party branches
      in Malaya and activities such as strikes. Demographic
      review, education, newspapers, the work of the protectorat

393. Lee Poh Ping. *Chinese Society in Nineteenth Century
      Singapore*. Kuala Lumpur: Oxford University Press, 1978.
      Pp. 139.

      A socio-political analysis, including discussion of the
      economic and political reasons for British control measure
      among the Chinese of Singapore and the nature of British
      over-rule.

394. Lim Teck Ghee. *Peasants and Their Agricultural Economy
      in Colonial Malaya 1874-1941*. Kuala Lumpur: Oxford
      University Press, 1977. Pp. 230.

      Dilemmas of government policy: on the one hand trying
      to protect peasants from threats to their holdings and
      on the other following a course that favors big estates
      over the long run, thus defeating the first aim. Malay
      reservations. Vulnerability of Malays in the face of
      Chinese superiority in commerce.

395. Lim Yew Hock. "Address to the British European Associa-
      tion, 26 July 1957, Singapore." *Malaya* (August 1957)
      20-21.

      By the chief minister, Singapore, three years before
      independence. Stresses the loyalty of the straits Chinese
      to Malaya and the record of racial harmony throughout
      the colonial period. Criticizes the British for disliking
      political activity in their colonies and points out that
      nation-building is always turbulent.

396. *Middlebrook, S.M. "Pulai: An Early Chinese Settlement
      in Kelantan." *JMBRAS* 11:151-156.

      Nothing is known of the origins of the settlement.
      Describes the population, languages, economy. The isola-
      tion of former times has ended.

397. ―――. "Yap Ah Loy." *JMBRAS* 24:12-127.

      The story of the best-known captian China in Selangor,
      the founder of Kuala Lumpur and a prime mover in tin

mining. An informative account of relations among British,
Malays and Chinese in the 1870s when British control was
extended to Selangor.

398. Neelakandha Aiyer, K.A. *Indian Problems in Malaya*. Kuala
      Lumpur: Indian Office, 1938. Pp. 150.

      Asserts that Indians in Malaya are much less free than
      Chinese because the former have not learned the art of
      organizing. Does not look to India for support in advancing
      the cause of Malaya's Indian community because India is
      "politician-ridden." The Labor Department of the MCS
      will lose its purpose when the workers unionize.

399. Neill, J.D.H. *Elegant Flower*. London: Murray, 1956.
      Pp. 202.

      A backward glance at the Chinese Protectorate by a post-
      1945 officer who was the last cadet to be sent to Amoy
      for language training. Highly informative on life in
      Amoy and in Malaya afterwards, on relations among the races.
      Critical of the Malay stream of the MCS for alleged dis-
      crimination against the Chinese stream.

400. Parmer, J.N. *Colonial Labor Policy and Administration: A
      History of Labor in the Rubber Plantation Industry in
      Malaya, c. 1910-1941*. Locust Valley, N.Y.: J.J. Augustin
      for the Association for Asian Studies, 1960. Pp. 294.

      British policy, methods and results. Helpful figures
      and tables. Covers both Indian and Chinese workers in the
      rubber industry.

401. *Pickering, W.A. "The Chinese in the Straits of Malacca."
      Fraser's Magazine 14:438-445.

      Chinese turbulence makes it necessary to keep a tighter
      rein on them than is strictly in accordance with straits
      laws.

402. ————. "Chinese Secret Societies and Their Origin."
      SBRAS 1:63-84.

      Beginnings of the societies in China itself and their
      transportation to the straits. Recruiting innocent youths
      on arrival in Malaya. Methods of the British in dealing
      with societies.

403. Price, I.R. *Annual Report of the South Indian Labour Fund
      Board*. Kuala Lumpur: Government Press, 1960. Pp. 35.

The fund was used for recruiting workers in India for
rubber estates in Malaya. Contributions were made by
employers, while government officers provided supervision.

404.   *Purcell, V. *The Chinese in Malaya*. Kuala Lumpur: Oxford
         University Press, 1948. Pp. 327.

         The history of immigration, British policy and the work-
         ing of the protectorate branch of the MCS, figures and
         tables on origins of immigrants and on the life of the
         Chinese in Malaya.

405.   ————. "Chinese Settlement in Malacca." *JMBRAS* 20:115-
         125.

         Chinese trade with Malacca, early settlement and agri-
         culture, from the fifteenth century forward. The role of
         the British in making the straits safe for immigrants.

406.   Raja Singam, Durai. *India and Malaya Through the Ages*.
         Singapore: Liang Brothers, 1954. Pp. 132.

         Relations between the two countries from the pre-
         colonial period onward. Trade, settlement, recruiting
         of labor.

407.   Sandhu, K.S. *Indians in Malaya*. London: Cambridge, 1969.
         Pp. 346.

         London dissertation. Origins of the immigrants, reasons
         for coming, methods of recruitment, work in Malaya, em-
         ployers and the supervision of the Labor Department.
         Rising political consciousness. Figures, by regions and
         years.

408.   Song Ong Siang. *One Hundred Years History of the Chinese
         in Singapore*. Singapore: University of Malaya Press,
         1967, Pp. 602.

         From the early nineteenth century forward. Society, econ-
         omy, government, education. Leaders. Race relations.

409.   *Stirling, W.G. "Chinese Exorcists." *JMBRAS* 11:41-47.

         Watching men walk barefoot on live coals. Speculating
         on the meaning of such practices and how they relate to
         Chinese values more generally.

410.   ————. *Chinese Shadows*. Singapore: Kelly and Walsh,
         1914.

Stories of the Singapore Chinese by a long-time protectorate officer, married to a Chinese and having experience outside the government service.

411. ————. *Shadows on a Malayan Screen*. Singapore: Kelly and Walsh, 1926. Pp. 20.

A picture book. Drawings with explanations of the work.

412. Tan Cheng Lock, Sir. *Malayan Problems from a Chinese Point of View*. Singapore: G.H. Giat, 1947. Pp. 182.

A prominent straits Chinese speaks out on post-war politics and social relations and on British policy.

413. Tinker, Hugh. *A New System of Slavery: The Export of Indian Labour Overseas 1830-1920*. London: Oxford University Press, 1974. Pp. 432.

The Indian migrations world-wide. A normative view and a polemic against the British. The treatment of Malaya is slight.

414. Toynbee, A.J. "Chinese Immigration into Tropical Territories in the Pacific Area." *Survey of International Affairs* 3B (1926) 456-467.

An over-all survey relating the phenomenon to conditions in both China and the lands to which immigrants went.

415. *Turner, G.E. *A Guide to the Workmen's Compensation Ordinance 1952*. Kuala Lumpur: Caxton Press, 1953. Pp. 11.

By a member of the Labor Department.

416. ————. "Indian Immigration." *Malayan Historical Journal* 1:80-84.

A short tracing and explanation of the methods of recruitment, origins of the immigrants in India and work in Malaya.

417. ————. "A Perak Coffee Planter's Report on the Tamil Labourer in Malaya in 1902." *Malayan Historical Journal* 2:20-28.

An account by Henry A. Haviland, found in India by an Indian officer working with the MCS there. Annotation by the author.

418. Vaughan, J.D. *Manners and Customs of the Chinese in the Straits Settlements*. Kuala Lumpur: Oxford University Press, 1971. Pp. 126.

Written from notes made by the author while serving
as a police officer in the 1850s. Later a resident and
lawyer he was in the straits for forty-five years. First
published in 1879.

419. Ward, J.S.M., and *Stirling, W.G. *The Hung Society Or
      the Society of Heaven and Earth*. 3 vols. London: The
      Baskerville Press, 1925, 1926.

      Detailed account of the history, organization and life
      of one of the major secret societies functioning in Malaya

420. [*Wilson, Charles.] London. Royal Commonwealth Society
      Library. Charles Wilson papers.

      Account of the Indians in Malaya by a former controller
      of labor in the MCS, written in the form of a book review.

421. Wynne, M.L. *Triad and Tabut: A Survey of the Origin and
      Diffusion of Chinese and Mohammedan Secret Societies in
      the Malay Peninsula, A.D. 1800-1935*. Singapore: Govern-
      ment Printer, 1941. Pp. 540.

      By the head of the Perak police. The Chinese sections
      are largely superseded by entry 377.

422. Yen Ching Huang. *The Overseas Chinese and the 1911 Revolu-
      tion*. New York: Oxford University Press, 1976. Pp. 439.

      Arrival of small numbers of revolutionaries in Malaya
      in 1906 and after. Sun Yat-sen's activities in Japan and
      efforts to organize the Chinese outside China in support
      of the revolution. British responses in Malaya.

See also 9, 18, 20, 21, 22, 23, 29, 31, 32, 33, 38, 40, 44, 45,
      52, 55, 57, 60, 68, 74, 89, 91, 98, 102, 111, 130, 157,
      166, 167, 171, 174, 185, 187, 206, 207, 209, 229, 233, 248,
      262, 266, 339, 425, 428, 430, 433, 436, 437, 438, 439, 445,
      448, 449, 450, 452, 465, 478, 483, 489, 490, 491, 492, 495,
      499.

VII. WAR, INSURRECTION AND TERRORISM

423. Allen, J. de V. "Raja Mahmud of Selangor's Account of the
Perak War, 1875." *Peninjau Sejarah* 3:63-70.

Contemporary account of events following Britain's
intervention in 1874, together with an introductory note
which provides the historical context.

424. Allen, Louis. *Singapore 1941-1942: The Politics and
Strategy of the Second World War*. London: Davis-Poynter,
1977. Pp. 343.

Analysis of the thinking of strategists in England and
Malaya, the fighting itself and the reasons for the Japanese success.

425. Barber, Noel. *The War of the Running Dogs: The Malayan
Emergency 1948-1960*. New York: Weybright and Talley,
1971. Pp. 284.

The Chinese communist insurrection and the British
campaign to suppress it.

426. *Brown, C.C. *Mural Ditties and Sime Road Soliloquies*.
Singapore: Kelly and Walsh, 1949. Pp. 26.

Poems of internment, 1942-1945, by an MCS officer in
a Japanese camp.

427. Callahan, Raymond. *The Worst Disaster: The Fall of
Singapore*. Newark: The University of Delaware Press,
1977. Pp. 293.

British civil and military preparations for the 1941
attack by Japan, the campaigns and the Japanese conquest.
Holds that Malaya was not strong militarily and that this
was not the fault of the civil authorities.

428. Campbell, A.F. *Jungle Green*. London: Allen and Unwin,
1953. Pp. 214.

The campaign against the communist insurgents from 1948 onward.

429.   Carver, Field Marshall Sir Michael, ed. *The War Lords*. Boston: Little Brown, 1976. Pp. 624.

The chapter on Marshall of the RAF Lord Tedder, by Air Chief Marshall Sir Christopher Foxley Norris, maintains that Tedder, who served in Malaya, put the blame for the fall of Malaya in 1942 on the high command in Britain, not on the civil government in Malaya.

430.   Chapman, F.S. *The Jungle is Neutral*. London: Chatto and Windus, 1950. Pp. 435.

A personal account of the "stay-behind" forces that remained in Malaya throughout the Japanese occupation, 1942-1945. By a colonel who served in the MCS post-war.

431.   Chin Kee Onn. *Malaya Upside Down*. Singapore: Jitts, 1946. Pp. 208.

The Japanese occupation, 1942-1945, by an eyewitness.

432.   Clavell, James. *King Rat*. London: Michael Joseph, 1963. Pp. 396.

A novel based on life in a prisoner of war camp, Singapore, 1942-1945.

433.   Clutterbuck, Richard. *The Long, Long War: Counter-insurgency in Malaya*. New York: Praeger, 1966. Pp. 206.

By a major general and lecturer at Exeter University. Includes the political background and a discussion of events before the war which help to explain the insurrection.

434.   Donnison, F.S.V. *British Military Administration in the Far East 1943-1946*. London: HMSO, 1956. Pp. 483.

Includes a helpful treatment of events in Malaya during the war and immediately afterwards.

435.   *Fletcher-Cooke, Sir John. *The Emperor's Guest 1942-1945*. London: Hutchinson, 1971. Pp. 318.

An account of capture and prison life in Japan, by an MCS officer.

436. Great Britain. Straits Settlements Police. Special
     Branch. *Police Intelligence Journal, Review of Communist
     Activities in Malaya, 1936*. Singapore: Government Printer,
     1 January 1937. Pp. 6.

     The direction of Malayan Chinese by their superiors in
     China, internal organization, finance, infiltration of
     labor unions, crimes, political demonstrations, propaganda,
     British responses.

437. Gurney, Sir Henry. *Communist Banditry in Malaya*. Kuala
     Lumpur: Department of Public Relations, Government of
     Malaya, 1950. Pp. 11.

     Extracts from speeches. By the high commissioner of the
     time.

438. Hanrahan, G.Z. *The Communist Struggle in Malaya*. New
     York: Institute of Pacific Relations, 1954. Pp. 146.

     History of the Malayan Communist Party. Pre-war activi-
     ties. The Malayan People's Anti-Japanese Army during the
     war. Guerilla warfare against the Japanese during the war
     and against the British afterwards. Sees a stalemate.

439. [*Henderson, K.J.] Oxford. Rhodes House Library. (M) K.J.
     Henderson papers.
     The experiment in rehabilitation of Chinese during the
     insurrection, 1950s, at a camp in Perak. By an MCS officer
     who served as assistant secretary for Chinese affairs.

440. Hino, Iwao, and Raja Singam, S. Durai. *Stray Notes on
     Nippon-Malaysia Historical Connections*. Kuala Lumpur:
     Kuala Lumpur Museum, 1944. Pp. 164.

     By a Japanese professor and an Indian scholar in Malaya.
     Written and published during the Japanese occupation of
     Malaya. Foreword by the Japanese governor of Negri Sembilan.

441. Holman, Dennis. *The Green Torture*. London: R. Hale, 1962.
     Pp. 190.

     The story of Robert Chrystal, a planter who remained
     behind Japanese lines, 1942-1945.

442. Ienaga, Saburo. *The Pacific War: World War II and the
     Japanese, 1931-1945*. New York: Pantheon, 1978. Pp. 316.

     By a Japanese scholar who lived through the war.

443.   Leasor, T.J. *Singapore: The Battle That Changed the World*
       New York: Doubleday, 1968. Pp. 325.

       By a novelist. Useful on race relations in the conflict

444.   *Maxwell, Sir W. George. *The Civil Defense of Malaya*.
       London: Hutchinson, 1944.

       The part played by civilians during and after the
       Japanese invasion.

445.   Miers, R.C.H. *Shoot to Kill*. London: Faber, 1959. Pp.
       215.

       The communist insurrection and jungle warfare.

446.   Miller, Harry. *Menace in Malaya*. London: Harrap, 1954.
       Pp. 248.

       The communist insurrection and its pre-war background.
       By an administrative officer who served in Malaya after
       the war.

447.   Parfitt, Iris. *Jailbird Jottings: The Impressions of a
       Singapore Internee*. Kuala Lumpur: The Economy Printers,
       1947. Pp. 84.

       About the women's camps in Singapore during the Japanes
       occupation, 1942-1945.

448.   Parkinson, C.N. *Templer in Malaya*. Singapore: Donald
       Moore, 1954. Pp. 39.

       A tribute to the high commissioner who supervised the
       suppression of the communist insurrection in the 1950s.

449.   Pye, L.W. *Guerilla Communism in Malaya: Its Social and
       Political Meaning*. Princeton: Princeton University
       Press, 1956. Pp. 369.

       Studies of individual members of the Communist Party,
       their doctrines and lives, their parts in the insurrec-
       tion. The author interviewed members of the MCS as well
       as many participants in Malaya.

450.   Short, Anthony. *The Communist Insurrection in Malaya
       1948-1960*. New York: Crane, Russak and Company, 1975.
       Pp. 547.

       Origins of the revolt, groups involved, tactics, aims,
       early successes and the British response. Draws on docu-
       ments gathered in Malaya and on talks with knowledgeable

British officers, MCS and military. Maintains that it was a mistake to end the Chinese Protectorate of the MCS since this left the British without an adequate organization for dealing with a Chinese insurrection.

451. Thatcher, Dorothy. *Pai Naa: The Story of Nona Baker.* London: Constable, 1959. Pp. 184.

An account of life in the jungles of Pahang during the Japanese occupation.

452. *Thompson, Sir Robert. *Defeating Communist Insurgency.* New York: Praeger, 1966. Pp. 171.

Draws on the author's experience of Malaya and Vietnam.

453. Thompson, Virginia. *Postmortem in Malaya.* New York: Macmillan, 1943. Pp. 323.

An essay in a series by the Institute of Pacific Relations, with a foreword by Sir George Sansom. Maintains that the defeat of the British in Malaya may be explained in part by the inadequacies of her pre-war government there. Sansom disagrees.

454. Thorne, Christopher. *Allies of a Kind: The United States, Britain and the War Against Japan 1941-1945.* New York: Oxford University Press, 1978. Pp. 772.

Discusses the very different American and British experiences in the East, their war aims and campaigns and their dealings with one another. Absolves the civil government of Malaya from blame for the defeat in 1941-1942.

455. Tsuji, Colonel M. *Singapore: The Japanese Version.* Sydney: R. Smith, 1960. Pp. 358.

The campaign of 1941-1942 as seen by a Japanese officer.

456. [*Vlieland, C.A.] London. King's College Library, Liddell Hart Centre for Military Archives. C.A. Vlieland papers.

"Disaster in the Far East," a paper on the fall of Singapore, by an MCS officer who resigned a year before as secretary for defense. Argues that the defeat was inevitable by virtue of the fact that London emphasized the Middle East, wrote off Malaya itself in the event of a Japanese attack and thought Singapore impregnable.

See also 18, 54, 68, 77, 92, 117, 122, 183, 184, 187, 227, 229, 272, 283, 303, 327, 348, 356, 377, 421, 422.

VIII. MISCELLANEOUS
Including Popular History, Journalism,
Fiction, Natural Science and Antiquarianism

457.   Banner, Herbert S. *Wanted on Voyage*. London: Hurst and
       Blackett, 1933. Pp. 288.

       A novel about life aboard ships plying between England
       and the East in the inter-war years.

458.   Barr, Pat. *Taming the Jungle: The Men Who Made British
       Malaya*. London: Secker and Warburg, 1977, Pp. 172.

       Covers the west coast Malay states for the most part
       and concentrates on the 1870s to 1890s. Mainly on the
       British and the Malays, not the Chinese and Indians. Use-
       ful portraits of the early administrative officers and
       vivid accounts of their work.

459.   Bilainkin, George. *Hail Penang*. London: Samson, Low
       Marston and Company, 1932. Pp. 242.

       A light-hearted account of social life and work in
       Penang and on the mainland, by the editor of a Penang
       newspaper. Interesting views of the MCS and the planters.

460.   *Birch, E.W. "The Vernacular Press in the Straits." *JMBRAS*
       42:192-195.

       Reprint of an 1879 article by a newly arrived straits
       cadet.

461.   Bird, Isabel. *The Golden Chersonese and the Way Thither*.
       Kuala Lumpur: Oxford University Press, 1967. Pp. 384.

       Travels in the Malay states during the 1870s. Portraits
       of Bloomfield Douglas, Low and other officers and of Malay
       royalty. See also entry 480.

462.   *Bland, R.N. *Historical Tombstones of Malacca*. London:
       Elliot Stock, 1905. Pp. 75.

463. *Caldecott, Sir Andrew. *Fires Burn Blue*. New York: Long-
      mans, 1948. Pp. 222.

      Allegory by an MCS officer who became a governor. Stori
      of planters, civil servants and Malays.

464. ————. *Not Exactly Ghosts*. New York: Longmans, 1947.
      Pp. 213.

      Fictionalized narratives based on the author's MCS
      service in part and on country life in England. Ambiva-
      lence on a career in overseas civil service.

465. Chettur, S.K. *Malayan Adventure*. Basel: Mission Press,
      1948. Pp. 260.

      Impressions of Malaya after the Japanese surrender in
      1945, by a much-travelled Indian who had entree to the
      mighty and the humble. Interesting on race relations.

466. *Clifford, Sir Hugh. "Joseph Conrad: Some Scattered
      Memories." *The Bookman's Journal* 11:3-6.

      Clifford and Swettenham met Conrad on their return to
      England in 1895. They were enthralled by his writings
      on Malaya and other Eastern lands, though they were aware
      of his mistakes and the thin local knowledge that his
      stories were based on.

467. ————. *Since the Beginning*. London: Grant Richards,
      1898. Pp. 288.

      A tale of an Eastern land, based on the author's early
      service in Pahang.

468. ————. *Stories*. Ed. W.R. Roff. Kuala Lumpur: Oxford
      University Press, 1966. Pp. 225.

      Thirteen of the best-known Malayan stories, together
      with a most informative introduction that provides a
      profile of Clifford's life and career.

469. ————. *Studies in Brown Humanity*. London: The Richards
      Press, 1927. Pp. 264.

      Stories and fictionalized essays, first published in
      1898. Europeans in the East, the character of the Malays,
      inter-action of Eastern and European ways of thought.

470. *Dennys, N.B. "Breeding Pearls." *SBRAS* 1:31-37.

471. ————. "The Snake-eating Hamadrgad." *SBRAS* 1:99-105.

472. Eastwick, Mrs. Edgerton. *The Resident Councillor*. Singapore: Straits Times Press, 1898. Pp. 259.

    A novel, written from articles printed in the *Straits Times* and portraying civil service life in the straits settlements in the 1890s.

473. Hake, H.B. Egmont. *The New Malaya and You*. London: Lindsay Drummond Ltd., 1945. Pp. 107.

    Land and people, with special reference to post-war reconstruction, as viewed by a prominent businessman and member of the federal council.

474. *Harrison, C.W. *An Illustrated Guide to the Federated Malay States*. London: Malayan Information Agency, 1923. Pp. 370.

    First issued in 1910. Notes for travellers, motorists, hunters. Also covers trade and provides information on museums, entertainment and sport.

475. ――――. *The Magic of Malaya*. London: Lane, 1944. Pp. 240.

    Stories reprinted from newspaper articles, first published in 1916.

476. *Hawkins, G., and Gibson-Hill, C.A. *Malaya*. Singapore: Government Printer, 1952. Pp. 113.

    A picture book, with text by Hawkins, describing the land and the people.

477. *Hazelton, Eric. *A Touch of the Sun*. London: Cassell, 1933. Pp. 284.

    A novel on Malayan life, by a cadet of the inter-war years.

478. *Hervey, D.F.A. "A Trip to Gunong Blumut." *SBRAS* 2:85-115.

    A vivid picture of the Johore countryside, taken from a diary of the 1870s. British, Chinese, Malays, economy and daily life.

479. Hill, Anthony. *Diversion in Malaya*. London: Collins, 1948. Pp. 186.

    An incidental account of five years in the Federated Malay States, by an education officer, 1937-1942.

480.   Innes, Emily. *The Chersonese with the Guilding Off.*
       2 vols. in one. Kuala Lumpur: Oxford University Press,
       1974.

       First published in 1885. A rather sour view of daily
       life by the wife of an administrative officer in Selangor
       and Perak, written to counterbalance entry 461.

481.   *Innes, J.R. "Old Malaya Memories." *British Malaya* 1:81-
       84.

       Anecdotes, partly autobiographical, of MCS life in the
       1920s.

482.   Locke, Lt. Col. A. *The Tigers of Trengganu.* New York:
       Scribner's, 1954. Pp. 191.

       A sporting and scholarly treatment of life on the east
       coast after 1945, by a post-war member of the MCS. Hunting
       legends, superstition.

483.   Lockhart, Sir Bruce. *Memoirs of a British Agent.* New York:
       Putnam, 1933. Pp. 354.

       Life as a young planter in the 1920s. Society, adminis-
       trative officers, sport, race relations.

484.   ————. *Return to Malaya.* New York: Putnam, 1936. Pp.
       376.

       A book of travel and impressions of society in Malaya
       and other parts, including the Dutch East Indies.

485.   Maugham, W. Somerset. *The Complete Short Stories of W.
       Somerset Maugham.* 2 vols. New York: Doubleday, 1952.

       Includes tales of inter-racial society in Malaya during
       the inter-war years (e.g., "The Letter," "The Force of
       Circumstance," and "Neil MacAdam"), based on impressions
       gained in visits to Malaya and Borneo. Colorful carica-
       tures, many drawn from personal contacts with MCS families

486.   ————. *A Writer's Notebook.* London: Heinemann, 1949.
       Pp. 367.

       Includes a section on Malaya in 1929.

487.   *Maxwell, C.N. *The Control of Malaria.* Singapore: Kelly
       and Walsh, 1930. Pp. 77.

488.   ————. *Malayan Fishes*. Singapore: Methodist Publishing
House, 1922. Pp. 101.

Written to provide data for government fisheries program,
important to the food supply and to the economy. Excellent
plates.

489.   Moore, Donald and Joanna. *The First One Hundred and Fifty
Years of Singapore*. Singapore: Donald Moore, 1969. Pp.
731.

A light and entertaining treatment by authors with rich
local knowledge and experience. Sound on government and
history, society and trade.

490.   Peet, G.L. *Malayan Exile*. Singapore: Straits Times Press,
1934. Pp. 89.

Taken from a journal covering the years 1930-1933.
Household details, social life, race relations and differ-
ences in racial outlooks.

491.   Read, W.H. *Play and Politics: Recollections of Malaya by
an Old Resident*. London: Wells Gardner, Darton and
Company, 1901. Pp. 178.

Wide-ranging memoir by a prominent businessman with close
contacts in government and in all the main racial communities. Especially enlightening on British dealings with
Malay leaders in the 1840s and on to the years of British
intervention on the mainland.

492.   Robson, J.H.M. *Records and Recollections 1889-1934*.
Kuala Lumpur: Kyle, Palmer and Company, 1934. Pp. 207.

By a businessman who served briefly as an administrative
officer and later as a member of the first federal council.
Helpful on major figures in government and business from
the late nineteenth to the early twentieth century. Malay
reservations. The Duff syndicate. The decentralization
controversy.

493.   Sidney, R.J.H. *In British Malaya Today*. London: Hutchinson, 1927. Pp. 311.

A picture book, with commentary on land and people,
travel and trade.

494.   Sim, Katherine. *Malayan Landscape*. London: M. Joseph,
1946. Pp. 248.

An account of daily life on the Perak coast, by the
wife of a customs officer. 1930s. Rural society, farming,
village groups, the sea. Appreciations of Malays and
Chinese. The East and England contrasted. Thoughtful and
dispassionate.

495. [Stratton-Brown, W.A.H.] Oxford. Rhodes House Library.
     NA 332. W.A.H. Stratton-Brown papers.

     Memoirs of Selangor in the 1890s. Swettenham, Rodger,
     Charleton Maxwell and other well-known figures. Social
     life, sport, clubs. A Chinese miners' riot and its suppres
     sion. Hill stations.

496. Syers, Capt. H.C. "Shooting in Selangor." *British Malaya*
     7:186-188.

     By a police officer who served briefly in the Selangor
     administration during the 1880s. The first of two articles

497. Wicks, P.C. "Images of Malaya in the Stories of Sir Hugh
     Clifford." *JMBRAS* 52:57-72.

498. Wildman, Rounsevelle. *Tales of the Malayan Coast*. Boston:
     Lothrop Publishing Company, 1899. Pp. 347.

     Travel book by American consul-general in Hong Kong,
     on a journey from Penang to the Philippines. Favorable
     view of British rule, seen informally.

499. Wright, A., and Cartwright, H.A. *Twentieth Century Im-
     pressions of British Malaya*. London: Lloyd's Greater
     Britain Publishing Company, 1908. Pp. 959.

     History, commerce, people, government. Chapters by MCS
     officers such as Wilkinson and Elcum.

Part Two
Biographies

PART TWO

Biographies

Information was sought on each officer's career, together with
family background and education. For many reasons the data
are incomplete. Early straits settlements lists are erratic
in content, while those for the protected Malay states, 1874-
1895, are more so and are fewer in number. For some states no
lists covering the first years of British rule have survived.
Most Malay states officers were locally recruited in the 1870s
and 80s; many served for short periods and do not appear in
any official list.

Generally speaking, there will be a correlation between
an officer's prominence and the length of his entry. Those who
joined the MCS in 1945 or later are not included because lists
for those years do not provide the biographical details found
in pre-war compilations.* However, a large number of pre-war
officers served on into the post-war years, and their entries
include data on postings in both periods. In the aggregate,
therefore, the whole span from the mid-nineteenth century to
the 1960s is represented.

The usual alphabetical order is employed in the cases of
British officers. Malay officers appear as in civil lists,
some alphabetically by name and others according to such titles
and styles as raja and syed.

Abbreviations and terms

SD:	secretariat and district postings
SS:	the straits settlements (Penang, Singapore and Malacca)
FMS:	the Federated Malay States (Perak, Selangor, Negri Sembilan and Pahang)
UMS:	the unfederated Malay states (Johore, Kedah, Perlis, Kelantan and Trengganu)

*Also excluded are officers who were appointed before the war
but do not appear in the 1940 Civil List, the last one that
provides full biographical information.

Cadet:	refers to officers who entered the service by examination, were appointed by the secretary of state for the colonies in London, beginning in 1867, and were posted initially to the straits settlements. Some later served on secondment in the Malay states. After the federation of 1896, all administrative officers were appointed by the secretary of state and designated cadets.
Junior officer:	refers to officers appointed by the secretary of state, beginning in 1888, to posts in the protected Malay states.
Malay:	The Malay-speaking (largest) stream of the MCS
Chinese:	the stream of officers trained in various Chinese languages and grouped together as the Chinese Protectorate
Labor:	the stream of officers trained in Indian languages and grouped together as the Labor Department

Honors and decorations

MC:	military cross
CH:	companion of honor
MBE:	member of the order of the British Empire
OBE:	officer of the same
CBE:	companion of the same
KBE:	knight of the same
GBE:	knight grand cross of the same
CMG:	companion of the order of St. Michael and St. George
KCMG:	knight of the same
GCMG:	knight grand cross of the same
Kt.:	knighthood apart from those in orders of chivalry
CB:	companion of the order of Bath
KCB:	knight of the same
GCB:	knight grand cross of the same

Abdul Malek bin Yusuf, Tun Dato', b. 1899

Malay College.

Probationer, 1914. Malay officer, 1917. District postings,
FMS. MCS 1933. District judge, Selangor, 1946-48.
Mentri Besar (chief minister), Negri Sembilan, 1948-53.
Speaker of Parliament, 1957. Governor of Malacca, 1959-
67. Retired 1967.

Acton, Roger David, 1874-1959

Called to the bar, Middle Temple, 1915.

Cadet, FMS, 1896. Malay. SD, FMS, SS, UMS. Legal postings.
District judge, Seremban. Retired 1929.

Adams, Sir Theodore (Samuel), CMG, 1885-1961

Son of clergyman. King's School, Canterbury. All Souls
College, Oxford.

Cadet, FMS, 1908. Malay. SD, FMS, UMS. Resident, Selangor,
1932-36. Chief Commissioner, Northern Nigeria, 1937-43.
See also entry 290.

Adkins, Edward Cecil Stapleton, OBE, 1903-1963

Son of clergyman. Christ's Hospital. Exeter College, Oxford.

Cadet, SS, 1927. Chinese. Protectorate and education posts,
SS, FMS. Interned by the Japanese. Secretary for Chinese
Affairs, Singapore, 1948-50. Retired for medical reasons,
1952. See also entry 205.

Ahearne, Christopher Dominic, CMG, 1886-1964

  Our Lady's Mount, Cork. Trinity College, Dublin.

  Cadet, SS, 1910. Labor. SD, Labor postings, SS, FMS, UMS.
    Controller of Labor. Federal Secretary, 1935-39. Retired
    1939. War work in Colonial Office and India. Head of
    Malayan Planting Industries Employers' Association, 1947.

Ahmad bin Osman, b. 1900

  Malay College.

  Probationer, 1917. Malay officer, 1919. District postings,
    FMS. MCS, 1947. District officer, Klang, 1950. Retired
    1952.

Aldworth, John Richard Oliver, b. 1866

  Cheltenham College.

  Local appointee, Selangor, 1889. Malay. District postings,
    FMS. Controller of Labor. Resident, Negri Sembilan. Retired
    1920.

Alexander, Charles Shuldham, b. 1877

  Clare College, Cambridge.

  Cadet, FMS, 1900. Malay. SD. Financial postings. Treasurer,
    FMS. Retired 1927.

Alexander, Noel Lancaster, b. 1907

  Son of physician. Clifton College. Pembroke College, Oxford.

  Cadet, FMS, 1931. Chinese. Protectorate postings, FMS, UMS,
    SS. Malayan Establishment Office. Interned by the Japanese.
    Secretary for Chinese Affairs, Perak. Retired 1958.

Allen, Lucien Arthur, OBE, 1888-1971

  Merchant Taylors' School. St. John's College, Cambridge.

  Cadet, FMS, 1912. Malay. District postings, FMS, UMS,
    Brunei. Controller of Rubber. Interned by the Japanese.
    Retired 1945.

Allen, Morris Anthony Vermont, b. 1875

    Junior officer, Perak, 1895. Warden of mines, Perak, Selangor.

Allen, Percy Tothill, b. 1878

    Cambridge University.

    Cadet, FMS, 1902. Chinese. Protectorate postings, FMS, SS.
      Resident councillor, Penang. Secretary for Chinese Affairs.
      Retired 1933.

Amery, Geoffrey Julian, b. 1875

    Oxford University.

    Cadet, FMS, 1899.

Anderson, Sir John, GCMG, KCB, 1858-1918

    Son of superintendent of Gordon Mission, Aberdeen. Aberdeen
      University. Called to the bar, Grey's Inn.

    Home civil service, 1879. Colonial Office. Governor, straits
      settlements and high commissioner, FMS, 1904-11. Permanent
      Under-Secretary of State for the Colonies, 1911-16. Gover-
      nor of Ceylon, 1916-18.

Anson, Maj. Gen. Sir Archibald (Edward Harbord), KCMG, 1826-
    1925

    Son of Gen. Sir William Anson, Baronet. Royal Military College,
      Woolwich.

    Military service, Malta, England, Crimea, Mauritius. Lieu-
      tenant-Governor, Penang, 1867. Retired 1882. See also entry
      207.

Anthonisz, James Oliver

    St. John's College, Cambridge.

    Cadet, SS, 1883. Labor. Postings in Indian immigration
      offices. Legal postings. Author, *Currency Reform in the
      Straits Settlements*.

Arthur, James Startin Wills, b. 1881

Marlborough College. Balliol College, Oxford.

Cadet, SS, 1904. Chinese. SD and protectorate postings, legal postings, SS, UMS. Director-general, posts and telegraphs. Retired 1936.

Ashworth, William Haughton, b. 1899

Cadet, FMS, 1921. Malay. SD, FMS.

Aston, Arthur Vincent, CMG, MC, b. 1896

King's School, Chester. Queen's College, Oxford.

Cadet, SS, 1919. Malay. District postings, SS, UMS. Resident councillor, Penang. Retired 1951. See also entry 12.

Baddeley, Sir Frank (Morrish), KBE, Kt., 1874–1966

Liverpool Institute. Magdalene College, Cambridge. Called to the bar, Inner Temple.

Cadet, FMS, 1897. Chinese. SD and protectorate postings, SS, FMS. Colonial secretary, SS. Chief secretary, Nigeria. Retired 1930.

Bahaman bin Samsudin, b. 1906

St. Paul's Institution, Seremban.

Probationer, 1924. Malay officer, 1925. District postings, FMS. MCS 1937. Minister for national resources, 1957. Other ministerial posts. Retired from political life, 1969.

Bailey, Arthur Walter, b. 1873

Cambridge University.

Cadet, SS, 1896. Chinese. SD and protectorate postings.

Bain, Norman Kerr, b. 1883

Mill Hill School. Sidney Sussex College, Cambridge.

Cadet, SS, 1906. Malay. SD and legal postings, SS, FMS. District officer, Lower Perak. Retired 1934.

Baker, Alan Custance, MC, 1885–1969

Victoria College, Jersey. Calvin's College, Geneva. Keble College, Oxford.

Captain, World War I. Cadet, SS, 1908. Malay. SD, SS, UMS. British adviser, Kelantan. Retired 1941. See also entry 121.

Ball, Arthur Dyer, b. 1888

Oxford University.

Cadet, FMS, 1911. Chinese. District postings, FMS. Transferred to Hong Kong and later Ceylon, where he died in service.

Bancroft, Kenneth Humphrey, 1905–1943

St. Paul's School. Pembroke College, Oxford.

Cadet, FMS, 1929. Labor. Secretariat and labor postings, FMS, SS, UMS. Malayan Establishment Office. Japanese prisoner of war. Died in Thailand during the war.

Band, Robert William Ingram, b. 1907

Son of clergyman. Aberdeen Grammar School. Aberdeen University. Corpus Christi College, Oxford.

Cadet, FMS, 1932. Chinese. Protectorate postings, FMS, SS. Attached to Australian forces. Prisoner of war, Singapore and Thailand, 1942–45. Secretariat and ministerial service post-war. Retired 1957.

Barnes, Warren Delabere, b. 1865

Cambridge University.

Cadet, SS, 1888. Chinese. Protectorate, legal and district postings. Secretary for Chinese Affairs. Acting resident, Pahang.

Barrett, Edwin Cyril Geddes, CMG, b. 1909

Son of officer in Indian Political Service. Marlborough College. Jesus College, Cambridge.

Cadet, SS, 1931. Malay. SD and legal postings, SS, FMS,
UMS, Brunei. Prisoner of war, Thailand. British adviser,
Kedah. Retired 1957. Lecturer in Malay, School of Oriental
and African Studies, London University. Retired 1971.
See also entry 208.

Barron, Jacob Maurice, 1891-1972

Dublin High School. Dublin University.

Cadet, FMS, 1914. Labor. SD and labor postings, FMS, SS.
Controller of labor. Retired for medical reasons, 1942.
See also entry 209.

Barron, William Douglas, b. 1887

Gordon's College. Aberdeen University. Balliol College,
Oxford.

Cadet, FMS, 1911. Malay. SD, FMS, SS, UMS. General adviser,
Johore. Interned by the Japanese. Retired 1945. See also
entry 210.

Bartley, William, CMG, MBE, 1885-1961

Trinity College, Dublin.

Cadet, SS, 1908. Malay. SD, SS, FMS, UMS, Labuan. Acting
British adviser, Kelantan. Acting colonial secretary, SS.
Retired 1939. War Office during the war. President, muni-
cipal commissioners, Singapore post-war. Retired 1946.

Bassett, John Harold, b. 1896

Wallasey Grammar School. Glasgow University. Called to the
bar, Middle Temple.

Cadet, FMS, 1921. Malay. District and legal posts, FMS, SS.
Retired 1935.

Bathurst, Henry Charles, 1887-1929

Cambridge University.

Cadet, FMS, 1910. Labor. Labor and legal posts, FMS, SS
and India. Died while serving as controller of labor,
Penang.

Bathurst, Henry Walter

  Haileybury. Clare College, Cambridge.

  Junior officer, 1889. District posts, protected Malay
    states.

Beatty, David, b. 1876

  Cadet, SS, 1898. Chinese. Protectorate and districts posts,
    SS, FMS. Secretary, Chinese Affairs, SS. Retired 1927.

Beckett, Osborne, b. 1889

  Dublin University.

  Lieutenant, Royal Dublin Fusiliers, Cameroons, France, War
    Office. Cadet, FMS, 1912. Malay. District posts. Suicide,
    c.1930.

Belfield, Frederick, b. 1863

  Oxford University. Called to the bar, Inner Temple.

  Local appointee, Pahang, 1889. Malay. SD and legal posts,
    FMS. Legal adviser. Retired 1920.

Belfield, Sir Henry (Conway), KCMG, 1855-1923

  Son of Justice of the Peace, Devon. Rugby School. Oriel
    College, Oxford. Called to the bar, Inner Temple.

  Local appointee, Selangor, 1884. Malay. Secretariat and legal
    posts. Resident, Selangor, Perak. Special duty, Gold Coast.
    Governor, East African Protectorate and high commissioner,
    Zanzibar. Retired 1920. See also entry 126.

Bell, William Gregory, b. 1873

  Glasgow University.

  Cadet, SS, 1897. Chinese. SD and protectorate posts, SS.
    Postmaster-general, SS. Retired 1914.

Bellamy, George Cumming

  Trinity College, Dublin.

Local appointee, Perak, 1884. Malay. SD, Selangor.

Berkeley, Hubert, Indian Service Order, 1864-1942

Grandson of the Earl of Kenmare. Midshipman, Royal Navy,
1881.

Local appointee, police, Dindings, 1886. Malay. District
posts Perak and Selangor. War service, Middle East,
Sudan and India. District officer, Upper Perak, for more
than twenty-five years. Retired 1926.

Berrington, Arthur Tewdyr Davis, b. 1854

Clifton College. Christ Church, Oxford. Called to the bar.

Local appointee, magistrate, Selangor, 1890. Legal posts.
Chief magistrate.

Biddulph, John Percival, b. 1904

Son of brigadier-general. Oundle School. Peterhouse,
Cambridge.

Cadet, SS, 1926. Chinese. Protectorate and magistrate posts,
SS, FMS. Prisoner of war. Deputy commissioner for labor,
Malacca. Retired 1954.

Bingham, Roy Porter, CMG, b. 1903

Dungannon Royal School. Trinity College, Dublin.

Cadet, SS, 1926. Chinese. Protectorate posts, SS, UMS.
Prisoner of war. Resident councillor, Penang. Retired 1957.

Birch, Sir Ernest (Woodford), KCMG, 1857-1929

Son of first British resident, Perak. Elstree School. Harrow
School.

Colonial Office, 1876-78. Cadet, SS, 1878. Malay. SD, SS,
FMS. Resident, Negri Sembilan. Governor of Labuan and North
Borneo. Resident, Perak. Retired 1910. Wrote memorandum on
irrigation, 1898. See also entries 212, 460.

Birch, James Cortright, b. 1850

    Cadet, SS, 1872. Malay. SD, SS. Resident councillor, Malacca.

Birch, James Woodford Wheeler, 1826-1875

    Son of clergyman. Midshipman, Royal Navy.

    Ceylon Civil Service, 1846-70. Colonial secretary, SS.
    Resident, Perak. Killed in Malay revolt. See also entry
    213.

Bird, Gerald Leonard Forssteen, 1905-1945

    Son of clergyman. Christ's College, Cambridge. Madrid
    University.

    Cadet, FMS, 1929. Malay. SD, FMS, UMS. Prisoner of war.
    Died in Labuan.

Bird, Reginald, 1893-1971

    Central Secondary School, Sheffield. Merton College, Oxford.

    Cadet, SS, 1919. Malay. SD, SS, FMS, UMS. Accountant-general,
    SS. Interned by the Japanese. Retired 1945.

Birse, Arthur Louis, 1893-1975

    Heriot's.

    Cadet, SS, 1921. Malay. SD, SS, FMS, UMS. Interned by the
    Japanese. British adviser, Selangor. Retired 1949.

Bishop, James E., b. 1875

    Cadet, FMS, 1898. Malay. District posts, Pahang.

Black, John Alan, 1891-1979

    Glasgow High School. Glasgow University.

    Cadet, FMS, 1914. Chinese. Protectorate, labor and district
    posts, FMS, SS. President, municipal commissioners, Penang.
    Interned by the Japanese. Retired 1945.

Black, John Graham, b. 1896

Son of schoolmaster. Royal High School. Edinburgh University.

Officer, Cameron Highlanders, 1915-18. Cadet, SS, 1920.
Malay. SD, SS, FMS, UMS. Malayan Establishment Office.
Interned by the Japanese. British adviser, Perak. Retired
1951.

Black, Sir Robert (Brown), GCMG, OBE, b. 1906

George Watson's College. Edinburgh University.

Cadet, FMS, 1930. Malay. SD, FMS, SS. Prisoner of war.
Governor of Singapore, 1955-57. Governor of Hong Kong,
1958-64.

Blacker, Kenneth Anthony, CBE, b. 1910

University College, London.

Cadet, FMS, 1932. Labor. Secretariat and labor posts, FMS,
UMS, SS. Interned by the Japanese. Commissioner, lands
and mines. Retired 1966.

Blacker, Maurice Hal, CBE, b. 1904

University College, London.

Cadet, FMS, 1929. Chinese. SD and protectorate posts, FMS,
SS. Interned by the Japanese. Adviser, lands, Kedah.
Retired 1959.

Blackwell, Kenneth Ray, b. 1896

Shebbear College, North Devon.

Lieutenant, 1915-19. Cadet, FMS, 1921. SD, FMS, UMS. Official
assignee, FMS. Resigned during World War II. Lecturer in
Malay, School of Oriental and African Studies, London
University. See also entries 214, 293.

Blagden, Charles Otto, d. 1951

Dulwich College. Corpus Christi College, Oxford.

Cadet, SS, 1888. Malay. SD, SS. Retired for reasons of health,
1897. School of Oriental Studies, London. See also entries
15, 16, 351.

Bland, Robert Norman, CMG, 1859-1948

    Son of general. St. Paul's School. Cheltenham College.
      Trinity College, Dublin.

    Cadet, SS, 1882. Malay. SD, SS, FMS. Resident councillor,
      Penang. Retired 1910. Ministry of Pensions, London, 1917-
      20. See also entry 462.

Blelloch, Ian William, CMG, b. 1901

    Dumfermline High School. Edinburgh University.

    Cadet, FMS, 1926. Malay. SD, FMS, UMS. Interned by the
      Japanese. British adviser, Perak. Retired 1957. See also
      entry 294.

Blythe, Wilfred Lawson, CMG, 1896-1975

    Birkenhead Institute. Liverpool University. University of
      Grenoble.

    Captain, World War I. Cadet, FMS, 1921. Chinese. Protectorate
      and secretariat posts, FMS, SS, UMS. Interned by the
      Japanese. Colonial secretary, 1950-53. See also entries
      376, 377.

Bosanquet, G.A.I.

    Cambridge University.

    Assistant colonial secretary, SS, and private secretary
      to the governor, 1899. Nigeria, 1904-09.

Bourdillon, Tom Louis, b. 1887

    Oxford University.

    Cadet, FMS, 1911. Labor. Killed in action, World War I.

Bowen, Charles David, b. 1862

    "Cadet," Perak, 1886. Malay. SD, Malay states and FMS.

Boyd, Andrew Conor, b. 1905

    Son of clergyman. Eltham College. Trinity College, Dublin.

Cadet, SS, 1929. Malay. SD, SS, FMS, UMS. Prisoner of war. Died in Thailand.

Boyd, Robert, CMG, 1890-1976

Son of clergyman. Campbell College, Belfast. Trinity College, Dublin.

Captain, 1915-18. Cadet, FMS, 1913. Labor. SD and labor posts, FMS, SS, India. Director of co-operation. Interned by the Japanese. Retired 1948.

Boyd, William Ryder, b. 1887

Son of clergyman. Campbell College, Belfast. Trinity College, Dublin.

Cadet, FMS, 1911. Malay. SD, FMS, SS. President, municipal councillors, Penang. Retired 1938.

Bozzolo, Carlo Ferdinando

Italian citizen. Local appointee, Perak, 1880. Magistrate, Upper Perak.

Bradley, Benjamin Gerald, b. 1899

Eastbourne College. Royal Military College, Woolwich. Called to the bar, Gray's Inn.

Cadet, FMS, 1921. Labor. District and labor posts, FMS, SS, UMS. Retired 1935.

Brander, James McPherson, b. 1905

Son of officer in Indian Civil Service. Fettes. Edinburgh Academy. Oriel College, Oxford. London School of Economics.

Cadet, FMS, 1928. Labor. SD and labor posts, FMS, SS, UMS. Co-operatives. Prisoner of war, Sumatra and Singapore. Retired 1955.

Brant, Ronald Vickers, b. 1907

Portsmouth Grammar School. Trinity College, Cambridge.

Cadet, FMS, 1930. Malay. SD, FMS, SS, UMS. Killed in action, World War II.

Bresland, Charles William, b. 1878

Cadet, FMS, 1901. Malay. SD, FMS, UMS. Retired 1924.

Brewer, Frank M., CMG, OBE, b. 1915

Swindon Commonweal School. Pembroke College, Oxford.

Cadet, 1937. Chinese, Prisoner of war, Sumatra. Secretary for defense, 1957-59.

Brewster, Edward John, b. 1861

Local appointee, Perak, 1878. Malay. SD, FMS. Resident, Pahang, 1911.

Brewster, Frederick William

Local appointee, Lower Perak, 1884. District posts.

Bridge, Blacker Frank, 1891-1962

St. Columbia's College. Trinity College, Dublin. Called to the bar, Gray's Inn.

Cadet, FMS, 1914. Labor. District and labor posts, FMS, SS. Transferred to colonial legal service, 1937. Interned by Japanese. Retired 1945. Wrote, with Cochrane, on law for planters.

Broadrick, Edward George, b. 1864

Clerk, Office of Works, London, 1884.

Cadet, SS, 1887. Labor. District and labor posts, SS. Lieutenant Colonel, Singapore Volunteer Corps. Resident, Selangor. Acting chief secretary, FMS. Retired 1919.

Brockman, Sir Edward (Lewis), KCMG, 1865-1943

Son of clergyman.

Cadet, SS, 1886. Malay. SD, SS, FMS. Resident, Perak, Pahang. Colonial secretary, SS. Chief secretary, FMS. Retired 1920. Head, Malay States Information Agency, London, 1920-25.

Broome, Richard Neville, OBE, MC, b. 1909

  Son of lieutenant colonel, Indian medical service. Rugby
    School. St. John's College, Cambridge.

  Cadet, SS, 1932. Chinese. Protectorate posts, SS, FMS.
    Escaped to Ceylon during World War II. Returned to Malaya
    during Japanese occupation, with Force 136. Secretary,
    Chinese Affairs, 1953-54.

Brown, Arthur Vanhouse, b. 1873

  Oxford University. Called to the bar, Inner Temple.

  Cadet, FMS, 1896. Labor. SD and labor posts, SS, FMS, UMS.
    Judge, Johore. Retired 1927.

Brown, Charles Cuthbert, 1888-1972

  Marlborough College. Trinity College, Cambridge.

  Cadet, FMS, 1911. SD, FMS, SS, UMS. Resident, Pahang, Interned
    by the Japanese. Retired 1945. Lecturer in Malay, School
    of Oriental and African Studies, London, to 1957. See also
    entries 295, 296, 297, 298, 299, 426.

Brown, Forbes Scott, b. 1872

  Settlement officer, Perak, 1900.

Bruce, R.

  Aberdeen University.

  Cadet, 1934. Chinese. Retired for medical reasons.

Bruce, Robert P.

  Local appointee, Perak and Selangor, 1877. Discharged after
    investigation of irregularities, 1883.

Bryant, Alfred Thomas, b. 1860

  Tonbridge School. Wadham College, Oxford.

  Cadet, SS, 1883. Malay. SD, SS. Resident councillor, Penang.
    Retired 1917.

Bryant, George William, 1887–1969

Emmanuel College, Cambridge.

Cadet, FMS, 1910. Malay. SD, FMS, SS. Resident councillor,
Malacca. Interned by the Japanese. Retired 1945.

Bryson, Hugh Patterson, MC, 1898–1977

Son of linen merchant. Royal School, Armagh. Queen's University, Belfast.

Officer, World War I. Cadet, FMS, 1921. Malay. SD, FMS, UMS,
SS. Interned by the Japanese. British adviser, Negri
Sembilan. Retired 1951. Secretary, British Association of
Malaya, London, to 1968. See also entries 128, 294, 300.

Bull, Harold Robert, 1888–c.1978

Framlingham. Queens' College, Cambridge. Called to the bar,
Middle Temple.

Cadet, SS, 1911. Chinese. Secretariat and protectorate posts,
SS, FMS. Transferred to colonial legal service. Interned
by the Japanese. Retired 1945.

Burgess, Harry Astell, b. 1871

Junior officer, Perak, 1894. Malay. District posts.

Burnside, Edmund, b. 1863

Son of Sir Bruce Burnside. Dover College, Kent. Maison Riston,
Nancy.

Private secretary to chief justice of Ceylon, 1883–88. Junior
officer, Perak, 1888. Acting resident, Selangor, 1913.

Burton, William, b. 1884

St. Olave's, Southwark. Christ's College, Cambridge. Called
to the bar, Gray's Inn.

Cadet, FMS. 1907. Malay. District and legal posts, FMS, UMS,
SS. Puisne judge. Retired 1936.

Butler, Arthur

  Local appointee, Perak, 1883. District posts. Resident,
    Pahang, 1900. Died of pneumonia, 1901.

Cairns, W.W.

  Ceylon service, 1852–67. Lieutenant-governor, Malacca,
    1867–69. Retired 1869.

Caldecott, Sir Andrew, GCMG, Kt. Bachelor, CBE, 1884–1951

  Son of clergyman. Uppingham School. Exeter College, Oxford.

  Cadet, FMS, 1907. Labor. SD and labor posts, FMS, SS. Resi-
    dent, Selangor. Colonial secretary, SS. Governor, Hong
    Kong, 1935–37, Ceylon, 1937–44. See also entries 216, 463,
    464.

Calder, James, CMG, 1898–1968

  Woodside School. Glasgow University.

  Cadet, SS, 1921. Malay. SD, SS, FMS, UMS. In New Zealand
    during the war. Chief secretary, North Borneo, 1946–53.
    Retired 1953.

Campbell, Archibald, b. 1877

  St. Andrews University. University of Marburg.

  Cadet, FMS, 1901. Malay. District posts.

Campbell, Douglas Graham, CMG, 1866–1918

  Surveyor, public works department, Selangor, 1883. Appointed
    assistant district officer, Selangor, 1887. General ad-
    viser, Johore, 1910. Died in office.

Campbell, J.A.G.

  Local appointee, Selangor, 1883. District posts. Inspector
    of schools, Kuala Lumpur.

Canning, Hubert

Clifton. Brasenose College, Oxford.

Local appointee, Sungei Ujong, 1890.

Capper, Alfred Houston

Royal School, Armagh. Trinity College, Dublin.

Cadet, SS, 1883. Chinese. Protectorate and district posts, SS.

Cardew, George Eric, b. 1887

Cadet, FMS, 1910. Malay. District posts, FMS. Killed in action, World War I.

Carey, Thomas Falkland, 1903-1966

King's Hospital, Dublin. Trinity College, Dublin.

Cadet, FMS, 1926. Labor. Secretariat and labor posts, FMS, UMS, SS. Controller of labor, Johore. Prisoner of war, Thailand. Commissioner for co-operative development, Malaya. Retired 1955.

Carter, William

Cadet, SS, 1890. Malay.

Cator, Sir Geoffrey (Edmund), CMG, 1884-c.1973

King's School, Bruton. Selwyn College, Cambridge.

Cadet, FMS, 1907. Malay. SD, FMS, SS, UMS, Labuan, Brunei. Resident, Perak. Retired 1939. Head, Malay States Information Agency, London, to 1948. See also entries 217, 218, 219.

Cavendish, Alexander, b. 1878

Oxford University.

Cadet, SS, 1901. Malay. SD, SS, FMS, UMS. Director of co-operatives. Retired 1933. See also entry 130.

Chapman, William Thomas, b. 1876

  Cambridge University. Called to the bar, Inner Temple.

  Cadet, FMS, 1899. Chinese. SD, protectorate and magistrate
    posts, FMS, SS. Secretary, Chinese Affairs, FMS. Retired
    1927.

Chevallier, Harvey, b. 1861

  Local appointee, Negri Sembilan, 1890. Malay. District posts.
    Acting resident, Labuan and Brunei.

Churchill, William Foster Norton, 1898-1963

  Son of army officer. Cheltenham College. Sidney Sussex College
    Cambridge.

  Cadet, FMS, 1921. Malay. SD, FMS, UMS. Interned by the
    Japanese. British adviser, Kelantan. Retired 1953. See
    also entry 220.

Clarke, Lt. Gen. Hon. Sir Andrew, GCMG, CB, Companion, Order
    of the Indian Empire, 1824-1902

  Son of army officer, governor of Western Australia. King's
    School, Canterbury. Royal Military College, Woolwich.

  Military service in New Zealand, West Africa and England.
    Elective office in Australia. Governor, SS, 1873-75.
    Minister, public works, India. Inspector-general of for-
    tifications, England. Wrote on the straits settlements.

Clarke, Cecil Harry George, b. 1878

  King's School, Canterbury. Jesus College, Cambridge.

  Cadet, FMS, 1901. Malay. SD, FMS, SS. Resident councillor,
    Malacca. Retired 1935.

Clayton, George Edward, MC, b. 1896

  Cadet, SS, 1920. Malay. SD, SS, UMS. Suicide c.1932.

Clayton, Lewis Hare, b. 1872

  Son of clergyman. Cambridge University.

Cadet, SS, 1895. Chinese. Secretariat and protectorate posts. Secretary, Chinese affairs. Retired 1920.

Clayton, Reginald John Byard, b. 1875

Cadet, FMS, 1898. Malay. SD, FMS, SS, UMS. British adviser, Kelantan. Retired 1930.

Clayton, Thomas Watts, b. 1877

Pembroke College, Cambridge.

Cadet, FMS, 1900. Malay. Officer, Mesopotamia, World War I. SD, FMS, SS, UMS. British adviser, Kedah. Retired 1932.

Clegg, Ronald Parr, b. 1901

Ipswich School. Pembroke College, Oxford.

Cadet, FMS, 1924. Malay. SD, FMS, UMS. Service ended 1938.

Clementi, Sir Cecil, GCMG, 1875-1947

Son of judge in India. St. Paul's School. Magdalen College, Oxford.

Cadet, Hong Kong, 1899. Chinese. Colonial secretary, British Guiana, Ceylon. Governor, Hong Kong, 1925-30. Governor, SS, and high commissioner, Malay states, 1930-34.

Clifford, Sir Hugh (Charles), GCMG, GBE, Fellow of the Royal Geographical Society, 1866-1941

Son of Maj. Gen. Hon. Sir H.H. Clifford. Educated privately at Woburn Park.

Local appointee, Perak, 1883. Malay. Resident Pahang. Governor, North Borneo. Colonial secretary, Trinidad, Ceylon. Governor, Gold Coast, 1912-19. Governor, Nigeria, 1919-25. Governor, Ceylon, 1925-27. Governor, SS, and high commissioner, Malay states, 1927-29. See also entries 25, 26, 134, 135, 221, 222, 223, 224, 301, 302, 303, 304, 305, 306, 466, 467, 468, 469.

Cochrane, Charles Walter Hamilton, CMG, 1876-1932

Son of clergyman. Repton School. Merton College, Oxford.

Cadet, FMS, 1899. Malay. SD, FMS, UMS. General adviser, Johore. Resident, Perak. Chief secretary, FMS. Retired 1931.

Cocker, Thomas Bernard, b. 1898

Cambridge University. Called to the bar.

Cadet, SS, 1921. Malay. Secretariat and legal posts, SS.

Cockman, Herbert James, Distinguished Flying Cross, b. 1898

St. Paul's School. Merton College, Oxford.

Cadet, FMS, 1921. Malay. SD, FMS, UMS. Killed in action, World War II.

Codrington, Stewart, b. 1874

Cadet, SS, 1898. Malay. SD, SS. Retired 1925.

Coe, Thomas Perowne, MC, b. 1887

King Edward VI School, Norwich. Brasenose College, Oxford.

Cadet, FMS, 1910. Malay. Officer, World War I. SD, FMS, UMS. Director-general, posts and telegraphs. Interned by the Japanese. Retired 1945. See also entry 226.

Cole, Walter, 1907-1943

Paston School. St. Catherine's College, Cambridge.

Cadet, FMS, 1929. Malay. SD, FMS, UMS. Officer, Argyll and Sutherland Highlanders. Prisoner of war. Died in Thailand, cholera.

Colman, Eugene Ernest, b. 1878

Cambridge University. Called to the bar, Inner Temple.

Cadet, SS, 1902. Malay. SD, SS, FMS. Legal posts. Retired 1933.

Conlay, William Lance, b. 1869

Army officer, England, India. Perak Sikhs, 1893. Acting junio officer, 1897. Police posts. British agent, Trengganu, 1909 Police posts, FMS.

Coope, Arthur Egerton, b. 1888

  St. Edward's School. Keble College, Oxford.

  Cadet, FMS, 1911. Malay. SD, FMS, SS, UMS. British adviser, Trengganu. Interned by the Japanese. Retired 1945. Wrote on Munshi Abdullah. See also entries 307, 379.

Cooper, H.E.G.

  Son of general.

  Cadet, SS, 1878. Chinese. Resigned after inquiry into improprieties in Amoy, 1881.

Corry, Wilfred Charles Stewart, CBE, 1900–1974

  Cheltenham College. Wadham College, Oxford.

  Cadet, FMS, 1923. Malay. SD, FMS, SS, UMS. Prisoner of war. British adviser, Pahang, 1948. Retired 1953. Secretary, British Association of Malaysia and Singapore, London. Served in Kenya and Brunei after retirement. See also entries 27, 136, 227.

Coulson, Norman, 1891–1978

  Charterhouse. Pembroke College, Cambridge.

  Cadet, FMS, 1920. Malay. SD, FMS, SS, UMS. District officer, Seremban. Interned by the Japanese. Retired 1945.

Cowan, William, b. 1863

  Local appointee, Chinese Protectorate, 1881. Protectorate posts, SS, FMS. Agent in China for Transvaal government. Protector of Chinese, Selangor, Negri Sembilan, Pahang.

Cowgill, John Vincent, CMG, MC, 1888–1959

  Son of clergyman. Durham School. All Souls College, Oxford.

  Cadet, FMS, 1911. Chinese. Service, World War I. SD and protectorate posts, FMS, UMS. British resident, Negri Sembilan. Interned by the Japanese. Retired 1945.

Cox, Francis Bede Simon, b. 1864

  Junior officer, Perak, 1888. District posts, FMS.

Crawford, John Gerald, 1894-1954

  King's School, Chester. Merton College, Oxford.

  Cadet, FMS, 1921. Malay. SD, FMS, UMS. Interned by the
    Japanese. Director of co-operation. Retired 1948.

Creer, John Kelly, OBE, b. 1908

  Liverpool Institute. Brasenose College, Oxford.

  Cadet 1932. Malay. District posts, FMS. Behind Japanese
    lines with Malayan People's Anti-Japanese Army. District
    officer, Kinta. Retired 1957.

Crichton, Reginald, b. 1877

  Cadet, FMS, 1900. Malay. SD, FMS, SS, UMS.

Cromwell, Tom Pearson, OBE, 1909-1976

  Son of industrial chemist. Grange High School, Bradford.
    Christ's College, Cambridge.

  Cadet, SS, 1932. Chinese. Protectorate and secretariat posts,
    SS, UMS. Interned by the Japanese. Director, social wel-
    fare, Singapore. Retired 1959.

Crum Ewing, Neil Robson, b. 1874

  Cambridge University.

  Cadet, FMS, 1897. Malay. District posts, FMS.

Cunyngham-Brown, John Sjovald Hoseason, OBE, b. 1905

  Son of physician. Blundell's School.

  Cadet, FMS, 1930. Labor. Labor posts, FMS, UMS. Prisoner
    of war. Consul in Thailand. SD, FMS, UMS, SS. President,
    municipal commissioners, Penang. Retired 1956. Consul-
    general of France, Penang, after retirement. See also
    entries 33, 229.

Curtis, Richard John Froude, b. 1897

   Blundell's. Royal Military College, Woolwich.

   Cadet, SS, 1920. Malay. SD, SS, FMS, UMS. Interned by the
   Japanese. British adviser. Trengganu. Retired 1953.
   Controller to household of sultan of Selangor.

Cussen, Richard Cyril, b. 1887

   Christian School, Cork. Trinity College, Dublin. Called to
   the bar, Gray's Inn.

   Cadet, FMS, 1911. Malay. SD, FMS, SS. Transferred to colonial
   legal service.

Dakers, Colin Hugh, MC, 1897–1942

   Manchester Grammar School.

   Army officer, World War I. Cadet, FMS, 1920. Chinese. Protectorate posts, FMS, SS. Prisoner of war. Executed by the
   Japanese.

Daly, Maurice Dominic, b. 1875

   Called to the bar, Middle Temple.

   Cadet, FMS, 1898. Malay. SD, legal posts, FMS, UMS. Retired
   1930.

David, Sir Edgeworth (Beresford), KBE, CMG, 1908–1965

   St. Edmunds School, Canterbury. Jesus College, Cambridge.

   Cadet, FMS, 1931. Malay. SD, FMS, SS. Prisoner of war in
   Korea. Ministerial posts after 1945. Colonial Office,
   1953. Colonial secretary, Hong Kong, 1955. Chief secretary, Singapore, 1958. Administrator, East African high
   commission, 1959. Retired 1962.

David, Paul August Felix, b. 1874

   Oxford University. Called to the bar, Middle Temple.

   Cadet, FMS, 1896. Chinese. SD and legal posts, FMS, SS.

Davidson, James Guthrie, c.1838-1891

  Practiced law, Singapore, 1861 ff. Resident, Selangor,
    1875. Resident, Perak, 1876-77.

Davis, Bernard Stratton, OBE, b. 1904

  Son of clergyman. St. John's School, Leatherhead. Keble
    College, Oxford.

  Cadet, SS, 1928. Chinese. Protectorate posts, SS, FMS, UMS.
    Interned by the Japanese. Secretary, Chinese Affairs,
    Perak. Retired 1953. Died 1970s.

Davis, Geoffrey William, 1906-1971

  City of London School. Lincoln College, Oxford.

  Cadet, SS, 1931. Chinese. Protectorate posts, SS, FMS.
    Interned by the Japanese. Permanent secretary, ministry
    of labor and welfare. Retired 1957.

Davis, Leslie Harold Newsom, CMG, b. 1909

  Marlborough College. Trinity College, Cambridge.

  Cadet, SS, 1932. Malay. SD, SS, FMS, UMS. Interned by the
    Japanese. Ministerial posts. Permanent secretary, ministry
    of communications and works, Singapore. Retired 1957.
    Special representative, Rubber Growers Association, in
    Malaya, 1958-63.

Dawson, Christopher William, CMG, b. 1896

  Son of clergyman. Dulwich College. Brasenose College, Oxford.
    Called to the bar, Gray's Inn.

  Army officer, World War I. Cadet, SS, 1920. Malay. SD, SS,
    UMS. British adviser, Perlis. Secretary for defense. In-
    terned by the Japanese. Chief secretary, Sarawak, after
    the war. Retired 1950. Deputy chief secretary, Eritrea,
    1951-52.

Day, Edward Victor Grace, CMG, 1896-1968

  Timaru High School. Christ's College, Christchurch, New
    Zealand.

Cadet, SS, 1921. Malay. SD, SS, UMS, FMS. British adviser, Perlis. Served in Cocos Islands during World War II. British adviser, Kedah. Retired 1952.

Del Tufo, Sir (Morobce) Vincent, KBE, CMG, 1901-1961

Son of European nobleman. Royal College, Colombo. Trinity College, Cambridge. Called to the bar, Inner Temple.

Cadet, FMS, 1923. Labor. SD and labor posts, FMS, SS. Interned by the Japanese. Chief secretary, Singapore. Retired 1952.

De Mornay, Frederick A.

Local appointee, Perak, 1884.

Dennys, Nicholas Belfield, Ph.D.

Postmaster's department, Royal Navy, 1855. Student interpreter, Peking. Acting vice consul, Tientsin, Canton, Amoy. Editor, *China Mail*. Assistant protector of Chinese, Singapore, 1877. Resigned 1882. Later served as police magistrate and as protector of Chinese, North Borneo. See also entries 35, 308, 470, 471.

Desborough, Charles Ernest Maitland, b. 1865

Local appointee, secretary to resident, Pahang, 1890. District posts. Magistrate, Kuala Lumpur. Retired 1908.

Dew, Arthur Tomkyns, b. 1853

Midshipman, Royal Navy, 1869. Local appointee, public works department, Perak, 1881. SD, SS and Malay states. District officer, Lower Perak. Retired 1908. See also entry 36.

Dickson, Eric Ayton, b. 1876

Son of Sir Frederick Dickson, colonial secretary, SS.

Junior officer, 1896. Malay. SD, FMS. British agent, Trengganu. District officer, Kinta. Retired 1931.

Dickson, Sir J. Frederick, KCMG, d. 1891

  Westminster School. Christ Church, Oxford.

  Cadet, Ceylon, 1859. Colonial secretary, SS, 1886. See also
    entry 37.

Dinsmore, William Holmes, b. 1877

  Trinity College, Dublin. Called to the bar, Inner Temple.

  Cadet, FMS, 1902. Malay. District and legal posts, FMS, SS,
    UMS. Judge, Kedah. Retired 1933.

Dodd, George Christopher, b. 1890

  Cadet, SS, 1914. Chinese. Secretariat and protectorate
    posts, SS.

Dohoo, Kenneth Godfrey Arthur, 1906-1944

  City of London School. Exeter College, Oxford.

  Cadet, SS, 1929. Malay. SD, SS, UMS. Prisoner of war. Died
    in Sumatra.

Donaldson, Charles Egerton, b. 1873

  Local appointee, Perak. Junior officer, 1893. Malay. SD,
    FMS.

Douglas, Francis William, b. 1874

  Son of Sir John Douglas, colonial secretary, SS.

  Junior officer, Perak, 1895. Malay. Officer, World War I.
    SD, FMS, SS, UMS. District officer, Klang. Retired 1928.
    Controller to household of sultan of Selangor after re-
    tirement. Wrote on historical geography of Malaya. See
    also entry 382.

Douglas, Sir John, CMG

  Rugby. Cheltenham College. University College, Oxford.

  Mauritius, 1859. Ceylon, 1869. Colonial secretary, SS, 1876-
    78.

Douglas, William Bloomfield, 1822-1906

　Merchant seaman. Captain of Raja Brooke's schooner, Borneo.
　　Government service, Australia. Acting magistrate, Singa-
　　pore, 1875. Resident, Selangor. Resigned 1882 after inquiry
　　into irregularities.

Dryburgh, Alexander Mitchell, b. 1895

　George Heriot's School. Edinburgh University.

　Cadet, FMS, 1919. Malay. SD, FMS, UMS. Transferred out of
　　Malaya.

Duberly, Frederick

　Cheltenham College.

　Local appointee, Perak, 1885.

Duckworth, Frederic Victor, CMG, 1901-1974

　Son of army officer. North Point School. Selwyn College,
　　Cambridge.

　Cadet, SS, 1924. Labor. SD and labor posts, SS, FMS, UMS.
　　Malayan agent in South Africa. Officer in Kenya during
　　World War II. British adviser, Selangor. Retired 1956.

Duff, Robert W.

　Police officer, Pahang, 1894. District officer, Selangor,
　　1900. Invalided out of service. Owned and operated exten-
　　sive mining and other concessions, Kelantan.

Dyson, Cecil Venn, b. 1873

　Cambridge University.

　Cadet, FMS, 1896. Malay. SD, FMS, SS.

Earl, Lionel Richard Franklyn, b. 1907

　Oakham School. St. John's College, Cambridge.

　Cadet, SS, 1930. Malay. SD, SS. FMS. Interned by the Japanese.
　　Secretary for education, Malaya. Retired for health reasons,
　　1955.

Ebden, Leonard Powney, b. 1864

  Cambridge University. Called to the bar, Inner Temple.

  Junior officer, Selangor, 1889. Malay. SD and legal posts, FMS, SS.

Ebden, William Sydenham, b. 1887

  Clifton College. Gonville and Caius College, Cambridge.

  Cadet, SS, 1911. Malay. SD, SS, FMS, UMS. Resident councillor, Malacca, 1940. Interned by the Japanese. Retired 1945.

Eckhardt, Henry Charles, b. 1877

  Cambridge University.

  Cadet, FMS. 1899. Malay. SD, FMS, UMS, SS. Acting British adviser, Kelantan. Retired 1932. Controller to household of sultan of Perak after retirement.

Edmonds, Robert Cecil, b. 1870

  Called to the bar, Inner Temple.

  Junior officer, Selangor, 1894. Malay. SD and legal posts, FMS.

Egerton, Sir Walter, KCMG, 1858–1947

  Tonbridge School. Called to the bar, Middle Temple.

  Cadet, SS, 1880. Malay. SD, SS, FMS. Resident, Negri Sembilan High commissioner, Southern Nigeria, 1903–04. Governor, Lagos, 1904–06. Governor, Southern Nigeria, 1906–12. Governor, British Guiana, 1912–17.

Elcum, John Bowen, 1860–1916

  Highgate School, London. Queen's College, Oxford.

  Cadet, SS, 1884. Malay. Chinese. SD, SS. Director of education, SS, FMS. Retired 1916. See also entry 499.

Eley, Hamar Joseph, b. 1894

  Military service, World War I. Cadet, SS, 1920. Malay. SD, SS

Ellerton, Henry Brooke, b. 1862

Local appointee, Pahang, 1892. Malay. SD, FMS. District
officer, Kuala Kangsar. Retired 1920. Malay States Imforma-
tion Agency, London.

Elles, Bertram Walter, b. 1877

Cambridge University.

Cadet, FMS, 1900. Malay. SD, FMS, SS. Resident, Perak.
Retired 1932.

Ellis, James William Condell, b. 1885

Cambridge University.

Cadet, FMS, 1908. Malay. SD, FMS. Died in service, c.1920.

Emeric, Fergus

Cadet, FMS, 1900. Malay. District posts.

Evans, Henry

Marlborough College.

Gentleman cadet, Australian mounted police, 1860. Local
appointee, immigration office, Penang, 1879.

Evans, William, 1860-1913

King's College, Cambridge.

Cadet, SS, 1882. Chinese. SD and protectorate posts, SS.
Resident councillor, Penang. Died in service.

Ezechial, Victor Gerald, b. 1883

Brother of Crown agent. King's College School, London.
Gonville and Caius College, Cambridge.

Cadet, FMS, 1907. Labor. SD and labor posts, FMS, SS. Retired 1933.

Faith, John Alexander Aelfred, b. 1903

  Son of army officer. Harrow School. New College, Oxford.

  Cadet, FMS, 1927. Malay. District posts, FMS, UMS. Interned
    by the Japanese. Retired 1945.

Falconer, John, b. 1898

  Aberdeen University.

  Cadet, FMS, 1921. Malay. SD, FMS, SS, UMS. Interned by the
    Japanese. British adviser, Johore. Retired 1952. See also
    entry 232.

Farrer, Robert Graves Blackburne, b. 1897

  Cadet, FMS, 1920. Malay. SD, FMS, SS, UMS. Killed in accident,
    1930s.

Farrer, Ronald John, CMG, 1873-1956

  Eton College. Balliol College, Oxford.

  Military service, World War I. Cadet, SS, 1896. Malay. SD,
    SS, UMS. Acting British adviser, Kelantan. President,
    Singapore municipality. Retired 1931.

Findlay, Charles Stewart, b. 1902

  Edinburgh University.

  Cadet, FMS, 1926. Malay. SD, FMS, SS, UMS. Retired 1934.

Firmstone, Harold William, b. 1868

  Cadet, SS, 1890. Chinese. District and protectorate posts,
    SS. Acting resident councillor, Malacca.

Fitzjames, Frank Arthur, d. 1893

  Clifton College.

  Cadet, SS, 1889. Chinese. Died of cholera.

Fleming, Edward Donovan, 1898–1972

 Bradford Grammar School. Jesus College, Cambridge.

 Cadet, FMS, 1921. Chinese. Protectorate and secretariat posts,
   FMS, SS, UMS. Interned by the Japanese. Secretary, Chinese
   Affairs, Malaya. Retired 1951.

Fleming, Thomas Cievers, b. 1863

 Canadian northwest mounted police, 1882–90. Police, Pahang,
   1890–93. Local appointee, Pahang administration, 1893.
   District posts, FMS.

Fletcher-Cooke, Sir John, Kt., CMG, b. 1911

 Malvern College. St. Edmund Hall, Oxford.

 Colonial Office, 1934. Cadet, Malaya, 1937. Malay. SD, FMS,
   SS. Prisoner of war, Japan. Colonial Office and colonial
   service, Palestine, Tanganyika, Cyprus. United Nations.
   Retired 1960. University appointments, United States. See
   also entries 383, 435.

Fonseca, Aloysius Hermenegild de Rozario, b. 1877

 Bombay University. Oxford University.

 Cadet, FMS, 1900. Chinese. Protectorate, SD, FMS. Financial
   and labor posts. Retired 1927.

Forbes, Leslie, b. 1889

 Son of clergyman. Appleby Grammar School. Queen's College,
   Oxford.

 Cadet, FMS, 1913. Malay. SD, FMS, SS, UMS. Resident councillor, Penang. Interned by the Japanese. Retired 1945.

Forrer, Henry Augustus, 1886–1969

 Dulwich College. Magdalene College, Cambridge. Called to the
   bar, Middle Temple.

 Cadet, SS, 1909. Chinese. SD and protectorate posts, SS,
   FMS. Transferred to colonial legal service.

Forsyth, Christopher Russell, b. 1910

  Ballarat High School. Melbourne University. Balliol College,
  Oxford.

  Cadet, 1936. Labor. District and labor posts, FMS. Joined
  Australian forces in Malaya. Prisoner of war. Secretary
  to treasury. Retired 1957.

Franklin, Alfred Edward Cyril, b. 1875

  Cadet, FMS, 1898. Malay. SD, FMS.

Fraser, Hugh, 1890–1944

  Wellington College. Exeter College, Oxford.

  Cadet, FMS, 1913. SD, FMS, UMS. Federal secretary, FMS. Interned by the Japanese. Died in prison.

Frost, Meadows, MC, b. 1875

  Charterhouse. Brasenose College, Oxford.

  Cadet, FMS, 1898. Malay. Military service, World War I.
  SD, FMS, UMS. Resident councillor, Penang. Retired 1930.
  Adviser in Sarawak.

Gammans, Sir David (Leonard), Baronet, Member of Parliament,
  1895–1957

  Portsmouth Grammar School. London University.

  Military service, World War I. Cadet, FMS, 1920. Malay.
  SD and co-operatives posts, FMS. Resigned 1934. Ministerial
  appointments, England. See also entries 46, 47, 138, 385.

Gates, Ralph Charles, b. 1906

  Son of physician. Westminster School. Christ Church, Oxford.

  Cadet, FMS, 1929. Malay. SD, FMS, SS. Co-operatives posts.
  Attached to Australian forces. Prisoner of war. Commissioner for co-operative development. Retired 1959.

Gatfield, William Herbert, MC, b. 1895

  Streatham Grammar School. St. George's College, London.

Military service, World War I. Cadet, SS, 1920. Chinese.
SD and protectorate posts, SS, FMS. Retired 1937.

Gent, Sir (Gerald) Edward (James), KCMG, DSO, OBE, 1895-1948.

Son of judge. King's School, Canterbury. Trinity College,
Oxford.

Military service, World War I. Colonial Office, 1920.
Assistant under-secretary of state. Governor, Malayan
Union, 1946-48. Killed in air accident.

German, Ralph Lionel, 1892-1968

Portsmouth Grammar School. Emmanuel College, Cambridge.

Cadet, FMS, 1921. Malay. SD, FMS, UMS. Interned by the
Japanese. Retired 1945.

Gibbes, Reginald Prescott

St. Edward's School, Oxford.

Cadet, SS, 1889. Labor posts.

Gibson, Sir Leslie (Bertram), Kt., Queen's Counsel, Bachelor
of Laws, 1896-1952

King Henry VIII School, Coventry. Called to the bar, Gray's
Inn. LL.B., London.

Cadet, SS, 1920. Malay. SD, SS, FMS, UMS. Transferred to
colonial legal service. Served in Trinidad and Palestine.
Chief justice, Hong Kong. Legal adviser to Foreign Office.
Retired 1951.

Gibson, William Sumner, CMG, 1876-1946

Son of clergyman. Marlborough College. Keble College,
Oxford. Called to the bar, Lincoln's Inn.

Cadet, FMS, 1899. Chinese. SD, protectorate and labor posts,
FMS, SS, UMS. Legal adviser, FMS. Retired 1935. Wrote
handbook for magistrates. See also entries 48, 71.

Gilman, Edward Wilmot Francis, CBE, 1876–1955

  Son of solicitor. Bradfield School. Brasenose College,
  Oxford.

  Cadet, SS, 1899. Labor. SD and labor posts, SS, FMS. Controller of labor. Resident councillor, Penang. Retired
  1931. Member, Oxfordshire regional planning committee. See
  also entries 233, 386.

Gilmour, Andrew, CMG, b. 1898

  Son of solicitor. Royal High School. Edinburgh University.

  Military service, World War I. Cadet, SS, 1921. Malay. SD,
  SS, FMS, UMS. Interned by the Japanese. Financial posts,
  Singapore. Acting colonial secretary. Retired 1953. United
  Nations posts. Secretary, British European Association,
  Singapore, 1956–75. See also entries 234, 235.

Glencross, Arthur, b. 1908

  Ashton-in-Makerfield Grammar School. Manchester University.

  Cadet, FMS, 1931. Malay. SD, FMS, SS, UMS. Prisoner of war.
  Commissioner, lands and mines, Johore. Retired for health
  reasons, 1954.

Glover, James Sands, b. 1877

  Cadet, FMS, 1901. Malay. District posts, FMS.

Goldthorp, Joss Wood, b. 1880

  Cadet, FMS, 1903. Labor. SD and labor posts, FMS. Died of
  dysentery.

Gompertz, Henry Hessey Johnston, b. 1867

  Oxford University. Barrister.

  Cadet, SS, 1890. Chinese. SD and protectorate posts, SS.
  Chief justice, FMS.

Goode, Andrew Nicholas, OBE, b. 1913

  Charterhouse. Trinity College, Cambridge.

Cadet, 1936. Malay. District posts, SS, FMS. Served in
Africa, World War II. Financial secretary, North Borneo.
Resigned, 1958, to join Commonwealth Development Corpora-
tion.

Goode, Sir William (Allmond Codrington), GCMG, b. 1907

Son of colonial civil servant, Rhodesia. Oakham School.
Worcester College, Oxford. Called to the bar, Gray's Inn.

Cadet, FMS, 1931. Malay. SD, FMS, UMS, SS. Prisoner of war.
Chief secretary, Aden, 1949-53. Singapore 1953-57. Governor,
1957-59. Chief of state, Singapore, 1959. Governor, North
Borneo, 1960-63. See also entry 236.

Goodman, Arthur Mitchell, 1886-1961

King Edward VI School, Bath. New College, Oxford.

Cadet, FMS, 1909. Chinese. Protectorate and secretariat
posts, FMS, SS. Resident councillor, Penang. Retired 1941.

Gordon-Hall, William Alexander, 1894-1964

Son of physician. Cheltenham College. Trinity College,
Oxford. Called to the bar, Gray's Inn.

Military service, World War I. Cadet, FMS, 1919. Malay. SD,
FMS, UMS. Interned by the Japanese. British adviser, Negri
Sembilan. Retired 1949. See also entry 237.

Gordon-Walker, Robin Ernest, b. 1886

Cadet, FMS, 1909. Malay. District posts, FMS. Retired 1919.

Gorsuch, Leslie Harold, CBE, b. 1897

Ipswich School. Sidney Sussex College, Cambridge.

Cadet, FMS, 1920. Malay. SD, FMS, SS, UMS. Interned by the
Japanese. Colonial Office and overseas posts after the war.

Gourlay, William Newlands, 1894-1978

Mountjoy School, Dublin.

Cadet, SS, 1920. Malay. SD, FMS, SS, UMS. Interned by the
Japanese. Commissioner, lands and mines, Malaya. Retired
1949.

Gracie, Alan James, CMG, 1904-c.1974

  Royal High School. Edinburgh University.

  Cadet, FMS, 1928. Malay. SD, FMS, UMS. Prisoner of war.
    Malayan Establishment Office. Federal establishment offi-
    cer 1954-57. Retired 1958.

Grant, Richard William, MC, b. 1897

  Cadet, SS, 1920. Malay. SD, SS, FMS, UMS. Interned by the
    Japanese. Retired 1945.

Gray, David, OBE, 1906-1976

  Carlisle Grammar School. Merton College, Oxford. London
    School of Economics and Political Science.

  Cadet, SS, 1930. Chinese. Protectorate posts. Interned by the
    Japanese. Secretary, Chinese affairs, Malaya. Acting chief
    secretary. Retired 1956.

Green, Charles Francis Joseph, b. 1875

  Cadet, SS, 1898. Malay. SD, SS, FMS. Resident, Pahang.
    Retired 1930.

Gregg, John Francis Fitzgerald, b. 1903

  Son of archbishop of Dublin. Shrewsbury School. Christ's
    College, Cambridge.

  Cadet, SS, 1928. Malay. SD, SS, FMS. Killed in action,
    World War II.

Grey, Robert Campbell, b. 1868

  Junior officer, Perak, 1888. Malay. SD, Perak and FMS.
    Secretary to resident, Selangor. Retired 1911.

Grice, Norman, 1893-1966

  Bradford Grammar School. St. John's College, Cambridge.

  Military service, World War I. Cadet, FMS, 1920. Chinese.
    Protectorate and secretariat posts, FMS, SS, UMS. Prisoner
    of war. Public trustee, Malayan Union. Retired 1947.

Grove, Oswald Harry, b. 1890

  Cadet, FMS, 1913. Malay. SD, FMS. Retired 1933.

Guillemard, Sir Lawrence (Nunns), GCMG, KCB, 1862-1951

  Son of clergyman. Charterhouse. Trinity College, Cambridge.

  Home civil service, 1888-1919. Chairman, board of customs
    and excise. Governor, SS, and high commissioner, Malay
    states, 1919-27. See also entry 152.

Haji Mohamed Eusoff bin Mohamed Yusoff, b. 1898

  Anderson School, Ipoh.

  Probationer, 1917. District posts, FMS. Assistant director
    of co-operatives. Retired 1948.

Hale, Abraham, b. 1854

  Local appointee, Perak, 1884. District posts, Perak and
    Selangor. See also entries 311, 312, 313.

Hall, Gilbert Amos, b. 1867

  Cadet, SS, 1888. Malay. SD, SS, UMS. Resident councillor,
    Penang. Retired 1922.

Hall, Julian Dudley, b. 1887

  Dulwich College. New College, Oxford.

  Cadet, SS, 1910. Malay. SD, SS, UMS. British adviser, Kedah.

Hallifax, Frederick James, b. 1870

  Cadet, SS, 1893. Malay. SD, SS.

Ham, Gordon Lupton, 1885-1965

  King Edward's School, Birmingham. Christ's College, Cambridge.

  Cadet, FMS, 1908. Malay. SD, FMS, UMS, SS. British resident,
    Negri Sembilan. Retired 1941.

Hammett, Harold George, b. 1906

St. Olave's School. Clare College, Cambridge.

Cadet, FMS, 1928. Malay. SD, FMS, UMS. Joined Royal Air
Force. Prisoner of war, Java. Resident councillor, Malacca.
Retired 1957. Commonwealth Relations Office and India.

Hamzah bin Abdullah, 1890-1971

Malay College.

Clerical service, FMS, 1908. Malay officer, 1918. SD, FMS.
MCS, 1921. District officer, Ulu Selangor. Retired 1941.
Political offices, Selangor and Malaya, 1946-63.

Hannyngton, John Forbes, b. 1906

Son of officer in Indian Civil Service. Charterhouse.
Trinity College, Dublin.

Cadet, FMS, 1930. Malay. SD, FMS, UMS. Prisoner of war.
British adviser, Trengganu. Retired 1957.

Hare, George Thompson, CMG, 1863-1904

Son of solicitor. Weymouth College. Shelborne. Wadham College,
Oxford.

Cadet, SS, 1884. Chinese. Protectorate and SD, SS, FMS.
Secretary for Chinese Affairs, FMS. Retired for health
reasons, 1904. See also entry 387.

Harris, Robert Christopher Skipworth, b. 1907

Son of clergyman. Monkton Combe School. St. Peter's Hall,
Oxford.

Cadet, SS, 1931. Labor. Labor and district posts, SS, FMS,
UMS. Killed in Persia during World War II while serving
as intelligence agent.

Harrison, Cuthbert Woodville, b. 1874

Cadet, FMS, 1897. Malay. SD, FMS. Under-secretary to government. Retired 1927. See also entries 155, 474, 475.

Hart, Morris Joseph, b. 1885

Oxford University.

Cadet, FMS, 1908. Malay. District posts.

Hart, Thomas Mure, CMG, b. 1909

Strathallan. Glasgow University. Brasenose College, Oxford.

Colonial Office, 1933. Cadet, MCS, 1936. Malay. District posts, FMS. Financial secretary, Singapore. Retired 1959. Bursar, Loretto School.

Harvey, John Allen, b. 1900

Christ's College, Christchurch, New Zealand. Otago University College. St. John's College, Cambridge.

Cadet, FMS, 1924. Malay. SD, FMS, UMS. Served in Nigeria during World War II. Resident councillor, Pahang (later British adviser). Retired 1955. See also entries 242, 314, 478.

Hashim Noor Mohamed, Indian Service Order, b. 1880

Penang Free School.

Student Malay interpreter, SS, 1898. MCS. SD, SS, FMS, UMS. Retired 1935.

Haughton, Hancock Thomas

Trinity College, Dublin.

Cadet, SS, 1881. SD, SS.

Hawkins, Gerald, OBE, 1891-1973

Son of clergyman. Marling School, Stroud.

Planter in Sumatra. Cadet, SS, 1920. Malay. SD, SS, FMS, UMS. Served in "Dalforce" during the war. Federal registrar of elections. See also entries 156, 476.

Hay, Alistair William, 1899-1944

  Tonbridge School. Exeter College, Oxford.

  Cadet, SS, 1921. Chinese. SD and protectorate posts, SS,
    FMS. Died of malaria in prison camp, Thailand.

Hay, Mortimer Cecil, b. 1891

  The School, Bishop Stortford. St. Catherine's College,
    Cambridge. Called to the bar, Middle Temple.

  Cadet, FMS, 1913. Labor. SD and labor posts, FMS, SS, UMS.
    British adviser, Perlis. Escaped from Malaya during the
    war. Governor, Seychelles. British Military Administration.
    Retired 1946. See also entry 243.

Haynes, Alwyn Sidney, CMG, OBE, 1878-1963

  Haileybury.

  Cadet, FMS, 1901. Labor. SD and labor posts, FMS, SS. British
    adviser, Kelantan, Kedah. Resident, Perak. Retired 1934.
    Lecturer in Malay, Oxford, and School of Oriental and Afri-
    can Studies, London. Wrote on agricultural subjects.

Hayward, Maurice John, b. 1906

  Son of officer in Indian Civil Service. Marlborough College.
    St. John's College, Cambridge.

  Cadet, FMS, 1929. Malay. SD, FMS, UMS. Prisoner of war.
    British adviser, Perlis, Trengganu, Pahang. Resident
    councillor, Malacca. Retired 1957. See also entry 244.

Hazelton, Eric, b. 1895

  Cadet, FMS, 1919. Malay. SD, FMS, UMS. Retired 1933. See also
    entry 477.

Headly, Derek, CMG

  Repton School. Corpus Christi College, Cambridge.

  Cadet, FMS, 1931. Malay. SD, FMS, UMS. Served in Palestine.
    Parachuted into Pahang, Spring 1945. British adviser,
    Negri Sembilan, Kelantan. Retired 1957.

Hellings, Geoffrey Stuart, b. 1888

Christ's Hospital.

Cadet, FMS, 1911. Chinese. SD and protectorate posts, FMS, UMS. Retired 1934.

Helps, Edmund Arthur Plunknett, 1888-c.1974

Marlborough College. Clare College, Cambridge.

Cadet, FMS, 1912. Labor. Served in East Africa, World War I. Labor and SD, FMS, SS, UMS. Retired 1933. See also entry 245.

Hemmant, George, CMG, 1880-1964

Tonbridge School. Pembroke College, Cambridge.

Cadet, FMS, 1903. Malay. SD, FMS, SS, UMS. Chief secretary, Nigeria, 1930. Retired 1934.

Hereford, George Arthur, b. 1875

Oxford University. Called to the bar, Lincoln's Inn.

Cadet, SS, 1898. Malay. SD, SS, FMS, UMS. Legal posts. Retired 1927.

Hervey, Hon. Dudley Francis Amelius, CMG, 1849-1911

Son of Rev. Lord Charles Hervey. Marlborough College.

Cadet, SS, 1867. SD, SS. Resident councillor, Malacca. Retired 1893.

Hewitt, Robert Douglas, b. 1857

Local appointee, SS, 1874. SD, SS, Malay states. Financial commissioner, FMS.

Heywood-Waddington, Alfred, 1898-1979

Son of clergyman. Devonport High School. Oriel College, Oxford.

Cadet, FMS, 1921. Labor. Labor and secretariat posts, FMS, SS, UMS. Interned by the Japanese. Federal economic secretary. Retired 1951.

Hill, Edward Charles Hepworth, b. 1854

Cadet, SS, 1875. Malay. SD, SS. Auditor-general, SS.

Hill, Thomas Heslop, b. 1850

Planter in Ceylon and Malaya. Recruiter of Indian labor
for Malayan estates. Served in public works department,
Selangor and Perak, 1880s. Protector of labor, FMS, 1901.
Retired 1905.

Hill, Valentine, b. 1866

Local appointee, SS, 1885. District posts, Malay states.
Resident, Negri Sembilan. Retired 1922.

Hodgkinson, John Douglas, 1907-1954

Son of officer in Indian army. Felsted School. Queens'
College, Cambridge.

Cadet, FMS, 1930. Malay. SD, FMS, UMS. Interned by the
Japanese. British adviser, Johore. Died in office.

Horne, William Donald, b. 1894

Aberdeen University.

Cadet, SS, 1920. Chinese. Protectorate and secretariat posts,
SS. Left the service, 1933. Returned for special duty,
1948-49.

Hose, Edward Shaw, CMG, 1871-1946

Son of bishop of Singapore. Blundell's School.

Junior officer, 1891. Malay. SD, FMS, SS. Colonial secretary,
SS. Retired 1925.

Howard, Edward Charles Clifford, b. 1868

Cadet, SS, 1890. Malay. SD, SS. Retired 1910.

Howitt, Charles Roberts, CMG, 1894-1969

Carlisle Grammar School. Queen's College, Oxford.

Cadet, FMS, 1920. Malay. SD, FMS, SS, UMS. Interned by the Japanese. Colonial Office. Malayan Establishment Officer. Retired 1950. Re-engaged 1951. Public service commission. Retired 1963.

Huggins, Sir John, GCMG, MC, 1891-c.1972

Bridlington School. Leeds University.

Military service, World War I. Cadet, FMS, 1920. Malay. SD, FMS, UMS. Malayan Establishment Office. Colonial secretary, Trinidad, 1938. Governor, Jamaica, 1943. Retired 1951.

Hughes, John Whitehouse Ward, b. 1883

Oakham School. Emmanuel College, Cambridge.

Cadet, FMS, 1906. Malay. SD, FMS, UMS. Resident, Negri Sembilan. Retired 1937.

Hughes, Trevor Davis, 1901-1945

King's College, University of London.

Cadet, FMS, 1925. Chinese. Protectorate, SD, FMS, UMS. Transferred to colonial legal service. Interned by the Japanese. Died of diabetes in camp. See also entry 54.

Hughes-Hallett, Humphrey Raymond, b. 1909

Taunton School. Queen Elizabeth's School, Crediton. Hereford College, Oxford.

Officer, Royal Air Force. Cadet, 1934. Malay. SD, FMS. Interned by the Japanese. Resigned 1945.

Hume, Lt. Col. William James Parke, CMG, 1866-1952

Son of officer in Ceylon Civil Service. Haileybury.

Junior officer, Perak, 1888. Malay. Military service, Boer War. SD, FMS. Resident, Perak. Retired 1921.

Humphrey, Arthur Hugh Peters, CMG, OBE, b. 1911

Son of bank manager. Eastbourne College. Merton College, Oxford.

Cadet, 1934. Malay. SD, FMS, SS. Resident, Labuan. Interned by Japanese. Malayan secretary for defense. Retired 1957. Commonwealth Relations Office. Retired 1961.

Humphreys, John Lisseter, CMG, CBE, 1881-1929

Bromsgrove School. Brasenose College, Oxford.

Cadet, SS, 1905. Malay. SD, SS, UMS. British adviser, Trengganu. Governor, North Borneo. Died while on leave in China.

Hunt, Harold North, 1894-1942

Ipswich School. St. Catherine's College, Cambridge.

Cadet, FMS, 1920. Malay. SD, FMS, UMS. Registrar-general of statistics.

Hunter, Sir John (Adams), KCMG, 1890-1962

Royal Grammar School, Newcastle-upon-Tyne. St. John's College, Cambridge.

Cadet, FMS, 1914. Labor. SD and labor posts, FMS, SS. Malayan Establishment Office. Lieutenant governor, Malta, 1938. Governor, British Honduras, 1940. Retired 1947.

Hussain bin Mohamed Taib, Dato', Orang Kaya Indera Shahbandar, Pahang, 1897-1949

Malay College.

Probationer, 1913. Malay officer, FMS. MCS, 1928. District officer, Temerloh.

Hyde, Anthony, b. 1900

Westminster School. Christ Church, Oxford. Called to the bar, Inner Temple.

Cadet, SS, 1924. Malay. SD, SS, UMS. Colonial Office, 1931-33. Returned to Malaya.

Ingall, Arthur Lenox, b. 1858

Rossall School.

Local appointee, Perak, 1888. Indian immigration agent.
SD, FMS.

Ingham, Raywood, b. 1889

Charterhouse. Corpus Christi College, Oxford.

Cadet, SS, 1912. Chinese. Protectorate and SD, SS. Retired
1933.

Innes, James

Treasurer, Sarawak. Collector, Langat, Selangor, 1877.
Resigned 1882.

Innes, John Robert, CMG, 1863-1948

Edinburgh University. Brussels University. Called to the
bar, Lincoln's Inn.

Cadet, SS, 1886. Malay. SD, legal posts. Judicial commissioner,
FMS. Retired 1919. Malay States Information Agency, London.
Wrote on census and legal subjects. See also entry 481.

Irvine, Robert, MC, 1894-1941

Dumfermline High School.

Cadet, FMS, 1919. Malay. SD, FMS, SS. Lost at sea, enemy
action, 1941.

Irving, Charles John, CMG, 1831-1917

Civil service, London, 1852-64. Mauritius. Auditor-general,
SS, 1867. Resident councillor, Penang. Retired 1887.

Isemonger, Edwin Empson

Home civil service, 1856. Transferred to SS, 1867. Resident
councillor, Malacca, 1891

Jago, Edward, b. 1898

   Cadet, FMS, 1921. Malay. Secretariat posts. Retired 1933.

Jakeman, Richard Wallace, OBE, b. 1908

   Altrincham County High School. Wadham College, Oxford.

   Cadet, FMS, 1931. Malay. SD, FMS, Labuan. Prisoner of war,
      Korea. Deputy commissioner-general, Malaya. Retired 1957.

James, Ernest Trevor, b. 1894

   Dublin University.

   Cadet, FMS, 1921. District posts, FMS.

James, Sir Frederick (Seton), KCMG, KBE, 1870-1934

   Son of army officer. Charterhouse.

   Nigeria, 1896-1916. Colonial secretary, SS, 1916-24.
      Governor, Windwards, 1924-30.

Jarrett, Norman Rowlstone, CMG, b. 1889

   Highgate School. Exeter College, Oxford.

   Cadet, FMS, 1913. Labor. SD and labor posts, FMS, SS, UMS.
      British adviser, Trengganu. Interned by the Japanese.
      Retired 1945. Secretary, British Association of Malaya,
      London. Wrote on land tenure. See also entry 247.

Jeff, John, 1896-1970

   Bellahouston Academy, Glasgow. Glasgow University.

   Cadet, FMS, 1920. Chinese. Protectorate and secretariat
      posts, FMS, SS. Interned by the Japanese. Commissioner
      for labor, Malaya. Retired for health reasons, 1948.

Jelf, Sir Arthur (Selbourne), Kt., CMG, 1876-1947

   Son of clergyman and master at Charterhouse. Marlborough
      College. Exeter College, Oxford.

   Cadet, FMS, 1899. Malay. SD, FMS, SS, UMS. War Office, 1918.
      Director, political intelligence bureau, Malaya. Colonial
      secretary, Jamaica, 1925. Retired 1935. Mayor of Hythe.

Jervois, Lt. Gen. Sir William (Francis Drummond), GCMG, CB,
   Fellow of the Royal Society, Royal Engineers, 1821-1897

   Son of general. Royal Military Academies, Gosport and
      Woolwich.

   Military service, England, Africa, Canada, Bermuda, India.
      Governor, SS, 1875-77. Governor, South Australia, New
      Zealand. See also entry 159.

Jervoise, Richard Somervell, b. 1887

   Bradfield College. Magdalen College, Oxford.

   Cadet, FMS, 1911. Malay. SD, FMS, UMS. Retired 1934.

Johnston, Lewis Audley Marsh

   Son of Member of Parliament.

   Derby School. Trinity College, Dublin.

   Cadet, SS, 1888. Malay. SD, SS.

Jomaron, Adolphe Charles, 1893-1963

   University College School. Corpus Christi College, Cambridge.

   Cadet, FMS, 1920. Malay. SD, FMS, SS, UMS. Interned by the
      Japanese. Commissioner for lands and mines, Malaya. Re-
      tired 1948. Served in Eritrea.

Jones, Nelson, MC, 1895-1951

   Glasgow University.

   Cadet, FMS, 1919. Labor. SD and labor posts, FMS, SS, UMS.
      Interned by the Japanese. Financial secretary, Singapore.
      Retired 1947.

Jones, Stanley Wilson, CMG, 1888-1962

   Hulme Grammar School. Manchester University.

   Cadet, FMS, 1911. Malay. SD, FMS, SS, UMS. Resident, Selangor.
      Colonial secretary, SS. Retired 1942. Served as consultant
      to Colonial Office afterwards. See also entry 160.

Jordan, Arthur Benjamin, b. 1890

Nottingham High School. Jesus College, Oxford.

Cadet, FMS, 1913. Chinese. SD, protectorate and labor posts,
FMS, SS. Secretary for Chinese Affairs, Malaya. Interned
by the Japanese. Retired 1945. Became clergyman. See also
entries 248, 392.

Joynt, Henry Raymond, b. 1888

Bradfield College. Balliol College, Oxford.

Cadet, FMS, 1911. Labor. Labor, SD, FMS, SS, UMS. Financial
secretary, FMS. Interned by the Japanese. Retired 1945.

Just, Albert Wolfgang, b. 1869

Junior officer, Perak, 1892. Malay. SD, FMS. Retired 1920.

Kamarudin bin Idris, Dato', b. 1904

Victoria Institution, Kuala Lumpur. Malay College.

Probationer, 1920. Malay officer. District posts. MCS, 1932.
State secretary, Trengganu. Mentri besar (chief minister).
Retired 1956.

Karl, Ernest

Chinese interpreter, SS, 1873. Assistant protector of
Chinese, Penang, 1877. Resigned 1885.

Kellagher, George Bannerman, b. 1889

Called to the bar, Middle Temple.

Cadet, SS, 1913. Malay. Served in France, World War I.
Secretariat posts, SS, UMS. Transferred to colonial legal
service. Interned by the Japanese. Retired 1945. Revised
laws of North Borneo after retirement.

Kemp, W. Cayzer

Local appointee, Pahang, 1889. Malay. District posts, Pahang
and Selangor.

Kempe, John Erskine, b. 1888

Radley College. University College, Oxford.

Cadet, FMS, 1911. Malay. SD, FMS, UMS. British adviser, Trengganu. Retired 1937. See also entry 249.

Kendall, Nevill, b. 1871

Oxford University.

Junior officer, FMS, 1895. Malay. SD, FMS, UMS. Adviser, land office, Kedah. Retired 1926.

Kennedy, Henry Albert, b. 1877

Worcester College, Oxford.

Cadet, FMS, 1900. Malay. District posts.

Keyser, Arthur Louis

Local appointee, Jelebu, 1888. Malay. District posts, Malay states. Consul, Brunei, 1901, after resignation from MCS. See also entry 251.

Kidd, George Montgomery, MC, 1889-1942

Tipperary Grammar School. Trinity College, Dublin.

Cadet, FMS, 1912. Malay. Major, Royal Irish Fusiliers, World War I. SD, FMS, SS, UMS. Resident, Selangor. British adviser, Kelantan. Missing in action, presumed killed during Japanese invasion.

King, Stuart Edgar, b. 1898

Merchant Taylors' School. St. John's College, Oxford.

Cadet, SS, 1921. Chinese. SD and protectorate posts, SS, FMS, UMS. In England during World War II. Director of immigration, Malaya and Singapore. Retired 1953.

King, Sydney Noel, b. 1897

Dover College. Bedford School.

Cadet, SS, 1920. Malay. SD, SS, UMS. Interned by the Japanese. Resident councillor, Penang. Retired 1948. Representative of Rubber Growers Association, Kuala Lumpur.

King-Bull, Eric James, b. 1897

  Officer in Royal Navy.

  Cadet, FMS, 1921. Malay. District posts, FMS.

Kingdon, Richard Claude Hawker, b. 1890

  Oxford University.

  Cadet, FMS, 1913. Killed in action, World War I.

Kingston, Thomas Walker Henry, b. 1887

  Trinity College, Dublin. Called to the bar, Middle Temple.

  Cadet, FMS, 1910. Chinese. Protectorate and district posts,
    FMS, UMS. Served in Burma. Retired 1928.

Kynnersley, Charles Walter Sneyd, CMG, 1849-1904

  Rugby School.

  Cadet, SS, 1872. Malay. SD, SS. Resident councillor, Penang.
    Retired 1904.

Laidlaw, George Muir, 1878-1919

  Cambridge University.

  Cadet, FMS, 1901. Malay. SD, FMS. Drowned near Pekan while
    serving as district officer.

Lambert, John Dirom, b. 1913

  Charterhouse. Magdalene College, Cambridge.

  Cadet, 1936. Labor. Labor posts, SS. Killed in flying
    accident, India, during World War II.

Langham-Carter, William, b. 1869

  Bradfield College.

  Cadet, SS, 1890. Malay. SD, SS. British adviser, Kelantan.
    Resident councillor, Malacca. Retired 1925.

Langston, Stephen Horatio, b. 1877

  Keble College, Oxford.

  Cadet, FMS, 1900. Malay. SD, SS, FMS. District officer, Kuala Kangsar. Retired 1931.

Laville, Louis Victor Joseph, 1888-1963

  Bedford School. Corpus Christi College, Cambridge. Called to the bar, Middle Temple.

  Cadet, SS, 1912. Malay. SD, SS, FMS, UMS. Transferred to colonial legal service. Interned by the Japanese. Puisne judge, Johore. Retired 1950.

Lawder, F.E.

  Sherborne School.

  Local appointee, Perak, 1881. Malay. District posts, Perak and Selangor. District officer, Kuala Selangor. Retired 1895.

Lee Warner, William Hamilton, OBE, b. 1880

  Rugby School. University College, Oxford. Called to the bar, Middle Temple.

  Cadet, FMS, 1903. Malay. Military service, World War I. SD, FMS, SS. Retired 1928.

Leech, John Bourke Massy

  Educated in Germany.

  Local appointee, Perak, 1880. District posts. Resigned 1895.

Leech, Chambré H.W.

  Dublin University. Civil engineer. Bachelor of laws. Called to Irish bar. LLD.

  Perak Police, 1877. SD, 1879 ff.

Leeds, Edward Thurlow, b. 1887

  Magdalene College, Cambridge.

  Cadet, FMS, 1900.

Lemon, Arthur Henry, CMG, 1864–1933

Son of barrister. Merchant Taylors' School. Exeter College, Oxford. Called to the bar, Lincoln's Inn.

Cadet, SS, 1888. Malay. SD, SS, FMS. Resident, Selangor. Retired 1920.

Lennox, William Wallace Mitchell, b. 1904

Spier's School, Beith. Edinburgh University. Wadham College, Oxford.

Cadet, FMS, 1929. Malay. SD, FMS, UMS. Retired for health reasons, 1939.

Leonard, Hugh Goodwin Russell, b. 1880

Bishop Cotton's School. Edinburgh University.

Cadet, FMS, 1903. Labor. SD and labor posts, FMS, SS, UMS. Resident, Pahang. Retired 1935. Wrote Telegu vocabulary.

Linehan, William, CMG, D.Litt., 1892–1955

Son of Irish senator. Christian Brothers College, Cork. University College, Cork.

Cadet, FMS, 1916. Malay. SD, FMS, UMS. Director of education, SS, adviser on education, FMS. Interned by the Japanese. Constitutional adviser, Malaya. Retired 1951. Research, oriental languages, Cambridge. Wrote on Thai–Malay relations. See also entries 164, 317.

Lister, Hon. Martin, 1857–1897

Son of third baron Ribblesdale, Cheltenham College.

Planter in Ceylon, Malaya. Local appointee, Perak, 1884. District posts, Selangor and Sri Menanti. Resident, Negri Sembilan. Died on leave. Wrote on laws and customs. See also entry 318.

Litton, George John Letablere

Eton College. Oriel College, Oxford.

Cadet, SS, 1891. Chinese. Transferred to consular service, 1895.

Lock, A.J.D.C., CBE, b. 1915

Imperial Service College, Windsor. Edinburgh University.

Colonial administrative service, 1937. Colonial Office.
MCS, 1941. Malay. Secretariat, Singapore. Prisoner of war.
Colonial Office. Malaya, 1946. SD. Secretary for commerce
and industry. Retired 1957.

London, Sir George (Ernest), Kt., CMG, 1889-1957

Warwick School. Downing College, Cambridge.

Cadet, FMS, 1911. Malay. Military service, World War I.
SD, FMS, SS, UMS. Under-secretary to government, FMS.
Colonial secretary, Gold Coast, 1935. Member of commission
of government, Newfoundland, 1944. Retired 1945.

Lornie, James, CMG, 1876-1959

Perth Academy. Edinburgh University.

Cadet, SS, 1899. Malay. SD, SS, FMS. Resident, Selangor.
Retired 1931. Wrote on SS land regulations.

Low, Sir Hugh, GCMG, 1824-1905

Educated privately.

Secretary to Raja Brooke, Labuan, 1848. Resident, Perak,
1877-89. See also entries 65, 168, 319.

Luckham, Harold Arthur Lee, b. 1904

Blundell's School. Balliol College, Oxford.

Cadet, FMS, 1928. Malay. SD, FMS, SS, UMS. Lt. Col., India,
World War II, after service in East Africa. Resident com-
missioner, Malacca. Commissioner of lands, Negri Sembilan.
Retired 1959. Served in West Irian. See also entry 254.

Lyle, Claude Wormald, 1913-1956

Sherborne School. Oriel College, Oxford.

Cadet, 1935. Chinese. Protectorate posts. Prisoner of war.
Secretary for internal affairs, Singapore. Died in office.

McArthur, Malcolm Stewart Hannibal, b. 1872

   Cadet, SS, 1895. Malay. SD, SS, FMS.

McCallum, Col. Sir Henry (Edward), GCMG, 1852–1919

   Son of army officer. Royal Military College, Woolwich.

   Inspector-general of fortifications, SS, 1874. Private
      secretary to the governor. Commissioner, Ulu Pahang, 1892.
      Governor, Lagos, 1897. Newfoundland, 1898. Natal, 1901.
      Retired 1907.

McCausland, Cecil Frank, b. 1872

   Captain, Essex Regiment. Junior officer, FMS, 1896. Malay.
      SD, FMS.

McClelland, Francis Alexander Stewart, b. 1874

   St. John's College, Cambridge.

   Cadet, FMS, 1896. Malay. SD, FMS, SS. Auditor-general, SS.
      Retired 1925.

McEvett, John Catherwood, 1906–1944

   Trinity College, Dublin.

   Cadet, FMS, 1930. Chinese. Protectorate posts, FMS, SS, UMS.
      Prisoner of war. Died of dysentery, Thailand.

Macfadyen, Sir Eric, Kt., 1879–1966

   Son of clergyman.

   Clifton College. Wadham College, Oxford.

   Cadet, FMS, 1903. Resigned 1905. Planter. Chairman, Planters
      Association of Malaya. Member of Parliament. See also
      entries 66, 169.

McFall, John Lynd, b. 1888

   Coleraine. National University of Ireland. Queen's College,
      Galway. Called to the bar, Middle Temple.

   Cadet, SS, 1910. Chinese. SD and protectorate posts, SS, FMS.
      Transferred to colonial legal service. Retired before the
      war. Returned afterwards, as judge.

MacGregor, Alexander Murray

> Collector, India, 1865. Protector of Indian immigrants, SS, 1880.

McKerron, Brig. Sir Patrick (Alexander Bruce), KBE, CMG, 1896-1964

> Son of professor. Fettes. Aberdeen University.

> Military service, World War I. Cadet, SS, 1920. Malay. SD, SS, FMS, UMS. Political secretary to commander-in-chief, Ceylon, World War II. Colonial secretary, Singapore, 1946. Retired 1950. See also entry 321.

Mackray, William Henderson, 1877-1919

> Oxford University.

> Cadet, FMS, 1901. Malay. SD, FMS, UMS. Died in service. See also entry 333.

McLean, Lachlan, b. 1877

> King's School, Canterbury.

> Cadet, FMS, 1900. Chinese. SD, protectorate posts, FMS, SS, UMS.

McNair, Maj. John Frederick Adolphus, CMG, 1828-1910

> Son of army officer. King's College, London.

> Indian army. ADC to governor, SS, 1857. Surveyor-general. Acting resident councillor, Penang. Retired 1884. See also entries 171, 322.

McNeice, Sir (Thomas) Percy (Fergus), Kt., CMG, OBE, b. 1901

> Son of clergyman. Bradford Grammar School. Keble College, Oxford.

> Cadet, FMS, 1925. Chinese. Protectorate, SD, FMS, SS, UMS. Prisoner of war. Chairman, commission on local government, 1955. Retired 1956.

Macpherson, Sir John (Stuart), GCMG, 1898-c.1972

Son of justice of the peace. George Watson's College. Edinburgh University.

Officer, Argyll and Sutherland Highlanders, World War I. Cadet, FMS, 1921. Malay. SD, FMS. Colonial Office, 1933. Nigeria, 1937. Palestine, 1939. War duties, United States and Caribbean. Governor and governor-general, Nigeria, 1948-55. United Nations, 1956. Permanent under-secretary of state for the colonies, 1956-59. See also entries 172, 255.

Macpherson, Lt. Col. R., d. c.1870

Resident councillor, Singapore, before 1867, while serving in Indian army. Colonial secretary, 1867. Died in office.

Mahmud bin Mat, Dato' Sir, KBE, CMG, 1894-c.1971

Malay College.

Probationer, FMS, 1912. SD, FMS. MCS, 1924. Member, constitutional conference. Retired 1948. Speaker, federal council. Mentri besar, Pahang. See also entries 173, 256, 323, 324.

Mahoney, W.J.

Local appointee, Perak, 1886. District posts.

Marks, Oliver, CMG, 1866-1940

Whitgift Grammar School.

Planter, Ceylon. Superintendent, government plantations, Perak, 1891. Malay. SD, FMS. Controller of labor. Resident, Selangor. Retired 1921. Secretary, British Association of Malaya. See also entries 69, 70.

Marriott, Sir Hayes, KBE, CMG, 1873-1929

Son of clergyman. Wyggaston School, Leicester. Sidney Sussex College, Cambridge.

Cadet, SS, 1896. Malay. SD, SS, FMS, UMS. Colonial secretary, SS. Retired 1928. See also entry 174.

Martin, Humfrey Trice, b. 1888

Cadet, FMS, 1912. Malay. District posts, FMS.

Martin, Sir John (Miller), KCMG, CB, Companion, Royal Victorian Order, b. 1904

Son of clergyman. Edinburgh University. Corpus Christi College, Oxford.

Dominions Office, 1927. MCS, 1931-34. Private secretary to the prime minister. Deputy under-secretary of state for the colonies. Retired 1965.

Mason, James Scott, 1873-1912

Son of gentleman, Isle of Man. Manchester Grammar School. Brasenose College, Oxford. Called to the bar, Lincoln's Inn.

Cadet, FMS, 1896. Malay. British adviser, Kelantan. Governor, North Borneo. Killed in riding accident.

Mather, Norman Frederick Hugh, 1890-1963

Merchant Taylors' School. Hertford College, Oxford.

Military service, World War I. Cadet, FMS, 1913. Labor. SD, labor posts, FMS, SS, UMS. Acting resident, Perak. Interned by the Japanese. Retired 1945.

Maundrell, Ernest Barton, 1880-1915

Cambridge University.

Cadet, FMS, 1903. Malay. SD, FMS, SS. Resident, Brunei. Shot by Sikh policeman.

Maxwell, Charlton Neville, 1872-1940

Son of Sir William Maxwell, MCS.

Served in Selangor and Sarawak and as private secretary to father when latter was governor of Gold Coast. Junior officer, Selangor, 1894. Malay. SD, FMS. British adviser, Trengganu. Retired 1927. Killed by driver when in retirement, Dindings. See also entries 325, 487, 488.

Maxwell, Sir William (Edward), KCMG, 1846-1897

  Son of Sir Peter Benson Maxwell, recorder, SS. Repton School. Called to the bar.

  Clerk to father, SS. SD, SS. Resident, Selangor. Colonial secretary. Governor, Gold Coast, 1895-97. See also entries 326, 327, 328, 329.

Maxwell, Sir (William) George, KBE, CMG, 1871-1959

  Son of Sir William Maxwell, MCS. Clifton College. Called to the bar, Inner Temple.

  Junior officer, Perak, 1891. Malay. SD, FMS, SS, UMS. Resident, Perak. Chief secretary, FMS. Retired 1926. See also entries 71, 176, 330, 444.

Megat Yunus bin Megat Mohamed Isa, b. 1906

  Malay College.

  Probationer, FMS, 1924. District posts. Chief assistant district officer, Kinta. Retired 1948.

Merewether, Sir Edward (Marsh), KCMG, Knight of Royal Victorian Order, 1858-1938

  Son of general. Harrow School. Called to the bar, Middle Temple.

  Cadet, SS, 1880. Malay. SD, SS. Resident, Selangor. Lieutenant-governor, Malta, 1902. Governor, Sierra Leone, 1911. Leewards, 1915. Retired 1921. See also entry 72.

Middlebrook, Stanley Musgrave, 1898-c.1944

  Bradford Grammar School. St. Catherine's College, Cambridge.

  Cadet, SS, 1921. Chinese. SD, protectorate posts, SS, FMS, UMS. Interned by the Japanese. Died in camp. See also entries 177, 396, 397.

Middleton, Charles Tyson, b. 1905

  Rugby School. Trinity College, Cambridge.

  Cadet, SS, 1928. Chinese. Protectorate and secretariat posts, SS, FMS.

Middleton-Smith, Richard, b. 1914

Wrekin College, Shropshire. Lincoln College, Oxford.

Cadet, 1936. Labor. District and labor posts, FMS. Prisoner
of war, Thailand. Deputy president, Singapore municipal
council. Retired 1958.

Miller, James Innes, D.Phil., b. 1892

Fettes College. Edinburgh University.

Cadet, SS, 1919. Malay. SD, SS, FMS, UMS. Interned by the
Japanese. British adviser, Perak. Retired 1948. Lecturer,
London University, Oxford University. Served in Tripoli-
tania and in ministry of overseas development.

Millington, William Milnes, b. 1883

Shrewsbury School. Manchester Grammar School. Corpus Christi
College, Oxford.

Cadet, SS, 1906. Malay. SD, SS, FMS, UMS. Resident councillor,
Malacca. Retired 1934.

Mills, John Vivian Gottlieb, D.Litt., b. 1887

Son of naval officer. Merton College, Oxford. Called to the
bar, Middle Temple.

Cadet, FMS, 1911. Chinese. Protectorate, SD, FMS, SS, UMS.
Solicitor-general, SS. Retired 1939. Honorary doctorate,
Oxford, for work on Chinese history. See also entries 73,
74.

Milverton, Baron (Arthur Frederick Richards), GCMG, 1885-1978

Clifton College. Christ Church, Oxford.

Cadet, FMS, 1908. Malay. SD, FMS, SS, UMS. Governor, North
Borneo, 1930. Gambia, 1933. Fiji, 1936. Jamaica, 1938.
Nigeria, 1943. Retired 1947. See also entry 258.

Mitchell, Sir Charles (Bullen Hugh), GCMG, 1832?-1899

Son of army officer. Royal Naval School, New Cross. Royal
Naval College, Portsmouth. Lt. Col., Royal Marines.
Colonial secretary, British Honduras, 1868. Receiver-

general, British Guiana, 1877. Colonial secretary, Natal,
1889. Governor, SS, 1893, and high commissioner, Malay
states, 1896. Died in office, 1899.

Mitchell, Walter Cecil, b. 1864

Son of clerk, Patent Office. Godolphin School, London.
Merton College, Oxford.

Cadet, SS, 1887. Malay. SD, SS, FMS. Resident councillor,
Penang.

Mitchell, William Walton

Godolphin School, Middlesex. Merton College, Oxford.

Local appointee, Pahang, 1889. District posts.

**Mohamed Razalli bin Haji Mohamed Ali Wasi, Dato', Muda Orang
Kaya Kaya Laxamana Perak, b. 1903**

Malay College.

Probationer, 1920. District posts. MCS, 1935. District
officer, Kuala Kangsar, 1950. Mentri besar, Perlis.
Retired 1955.

Mohamed Salleh bin Haji Sulaiman, MBE, b. 1904

Malay College.

Probationer, 1920. District posts, FMS. MCS 1933. Deputy
chief social welfare officer, Malaya. Retired 1957.

Moles, Hugh Graham, b. 1905

Crossley Schools, Halifax. Gonville and Caius College,
Cambridge.

Cadet, FMS, 1929. Chinese. Protectorate and district posts,
FMS, UMS. Service in Burma. Retired for health reasons
during World War II.

Monk, Harold Francis, b. 1890

St. George's School, Harpenden. Wadham College, Oxford.

Cadet, SS, 1914. Malay. SD, SS, FMS, UMS.

Moor, Richard, b. 1898

  Ermysted's School, Skipton. Hertford College, Oxford. Called
  to the bar, Middle Temple.

  Cadet, SS, 1921. Malay. SD, SS, FMS, UMS. Transferred to
  colonial legal service. Interned by the Japanese. High
  Court judge. Retired 1950.

Morkill, Alan Greenwood, OBE, b. 1890

  Charterhouse. New College, Oxford.

  Cadet, FMS, 1913. Malay district posts, UMS, FMS. Retired
  for health reasons, 1927. See also entry 259.

Morten, Frederick Joseph, CMG, 1888-1960

  Lancing College. Exeter College, Oxford.

  Cadet, SS, 1912. Malay. SD, SS. Director of education, SS,
  and adviser on education, FMS. Retired 1938.

Moubray, George Alexander de Chazal de, 1888-1977

  Loretto School. Manchester University. Zurich University
  and Polytechnikum.

  Cadet, FMS, 1912. Labor. SD, FMS, SS, UMS. British adviser,
  Trengganu. Prisoner of war. Retired 1945. See also entries
  260, 332.

Mudie, Norman David, b. 1884

  High School, Dundee. Edinburgh University. Called to the
  bar, Middle Temple.

  Cadet, SS, 1907. Chinese. Protectorate posts, SS, FMS.
  Judge, FMS. Retired 1935.

Muller, Gilbert Cornelius Grenon, b. 1888

  Oxford University.

  Cadet, SS, 1912. Malay. SD, SS.

Murray, Arthur

  Local appointee, Perak, 1889. Junior officer, 1890. District
  posts, Perak.

Murray, Patrick James, c.1837–1881

  Royal Navy, 1856. Retired, Captain, 1872. Acting assistant
    resident, Sungei Ujong, 1875. Resident. Died in Malacca,
    1881.

Muspratt, Colin Knox, b. 1893

  Military service, World War I. Cadet, FMS, 1920. Chinese.
    Protectorate posts, FMS.

Mustapha Albakri bin Haji Hassan, CBE, b. 1902

  Anderson School, Ipoh. Malay College.

  Probationer, 1921. Malay officer. District posts, FMS. MCS
    1935. State and royal posts. Retired 1957. Grand chamber-
    lain.

Nairn, Philip Sidney Fletcher, 1883–1914

  King's School, Canterbury. Trinity College, Oxford.

  Cadet, Kelantan service (under Siam), 1907. Malay. Transferred
    to FMS, 1910. District posts. Died in service. See also
    entry 261.

Nash, George Hutcheson, b. 1889

  St. John's School, Leatherhead. Queen's College, Oxford.

  Cadet, FMS, 1912. Malay. SD, FMS, UMS. Retired 1934.

Nathan, Julius Ernest, b. 1881

  Oxford University.

  Cadet, SS, 1904. Malay. SD, SS, FMS. Retired 1923.

Neave, John Richard, MC, 1893–1942

  City School, Lincoln. King's College, London.

  Cadet, SS, 1919. Malay. SD, SS, FMS, UMS. Acting resident,
    Perak. Killed in action, World War II.

Newboult, Sir Alexander (Theodore), KBE, CMG, MC, 1896-1964

Son of clergyman. Oakham School. Kingswood School. Exeter College, Oxford.

Cadet, FMS, 1920. Malay. SD, FMS, UMS. Colonial secretary, Fiji, 1942. Deputy chief, civil affairs office (Brigadier), 1945. Chief secretary, Malaya, 1946. Retired 1950.

Nightingale, Herbert Walter, b. 1908

Strand School. University College, London.

Cadet, SS, 1932. Labor. SD, labor posts, SS, FMS, UMS. Served in Africa, 1942-45. Deputy commissioner for labor, Perak. Retired 1957.

Norman, Henry, b. 1877

Cadet, FMS, 1899. Malay. SD, FMS, SS, UMS. See also entry 79.

North-Hunt, Harold, b. 1894-1942

Ipswich School. St. Catherine's College, Cambridge.

Military service, World War I. Cadet, FMS, 1920. Malay. SD, FMS, SS, UMS. Interned by the Japanese. Died in hospital.

Nunn, Bernard, b. 1876

Oxford University.

Cadet, SS, 1900. Malay. Chinese. SD, protectorate posts, SS. Retired 1927.

Oakeley, Rowland Henry, b. 1909

Son of army officer. Clifton College. New College, Oxford.

Cadet, SS, 1931. Chinese. Protectorate posts, SS. Interned by the Japanese. Commissioner for labor, Malaya. Retired 1958. See also entry 262.

O'Brien, Henry Arthur

Repton School.

Cadet, SS, 1875. Malay. SD, SS and Sungei Ujong. Postmaster-general, SS.

Ord, Maj. Gen. Sir Harry (St. George), Kt., CB

    Governor of Bermuda. Governor, SS, 1867-73.

Osborne, H.T.K.

    Foyle College, Londonderry. Trinity College, Dublin.
    Junior officer, Perak, 1889. District posts, Perak.

Osborne, R.B., MC

    Cadet, SS, 1909. Malay. Military service, World War I. SD,
      SS. Private secretary to governor, 1920.

Osman bin Talib, Tan Sri Datuk, b. 1906

    Anderson School, Ipoh.

    Probationer, 1925. Malay officer. District posts, FMS. MCS
      1938. State posts. Chief minister, Malacca. Retired 1957.
      Director-general, national electricity board.

O'Sullivan, Arthur Warren Swete

    Dublin University.

    Cadet, SS, 1883. Malay. SD, SS. Colonial secretary, Trinidad.
      Died in service. Wrote on relations between southern
      India and SS.

Oswell, Henry Theodore Warren, 1896-1972

    Son of naval officer. Dulwich College. Worcester College,
      Oxford.

    Cadet, FMS, 1920. Labor. SD, labor posts, FMS, UMS. Interned
      by the Japanese. President, municipal commissioners,
      Kuala Lumpur. Retired 1952.

Othman bin Mohamed, Dato', CMG, b. 1905

    Victoria Institution, Kuala Lumpur.

    Probationer, 1923. Malay officer. SD, FMS. MCS, 1935. State
      posts. Commissioner for Malaya, London. Permanent secre-
      tary, ministry for external affairs, 1957.

Ouston, Geoffrey, b. 1869

New College, Oxford.

Cadet, FMS, 1900. Malay.

Owen, John Fortescue, b. 1869

Blundell's.

Junior officer, Pahang, 1889. Malay. SD, FMS, SS. Commissioner of lands, FMS. Retired 1921.

Parr, Lt. Col. Cecil William Chase, CMG, OBE, 1871-1943

Son of colonial civil servant.

Junior officer, Perak, 1889. Malay. Military service, World War I. Resident, Perak. Retired 1926. See also entry 333.

Paterson, Henry Sibbald, b. 1890

Winchester College. Magdalen College, Oxford.

Cadet, FMS, 1913. Malay. Military service, World War I. SD, FMS, SS, UMS. Worked on enemy aliens in England, World War II. Retired 1945.

Patton, Thomas Watters, b. 1887

Dublin University.

Cadet, FMS, 1910. Malay. District posts, FMS.

Paul, William Francis Bourne, b. 1844

Eton College.

Served in Sarawak, 1860. Accra, 1873. Local appointee, Perak, 1876. Resident, Sungei Ujong, 1881. Retired 1893.

Pawanteh bin Haji Mohamed, b. 1888

Malay College.

Clerical service, FMS, 1906. Malay officer. SD, FMS. Retired 1940.

Peacock, Walter, b. 1875

  Cambridge University.

  Cadet, SS, 1898. Chinese. Protectorate and district posts,
    SS, FMS. Protector of Chinese, SS. Retired 1917.

Peck, Arthur Kenrick, b. 1876

  Cambridge University.

  Cadet, FMS, 1899. Malay. District posts, FMS.

Pedlow, Joseph Howard, 1889-1942

  Intermediate School, Newry. Queen's College, Galway. Called
    to the bar, Middle Temple.

  Cadet, SS, 1912. Chinese. Protectorate posts, SS. Transferred
    to colonial legal service. Disappeared c.1942; presumed
    lost as a result of enemy action.

Peel, Sir William, KCMG, KBE, 1875-1945

  Son of clergyman. Silcoates School. Queens' College, Cam-
    bridge.

  Cadet, SS, 1897. Malay. SD, SS, FMS, UMS. Chief secretary,
    FMS, 1926. Governor, Hong Kong, 1930. Retired 1935. See
    also entry 263.

Peel, Sir (William) John, Kt., b. 1912

  Son of governor of Hong Kong. Wellington College. Queens'
    College, Cambridge.

  Cadet, 1934. Malay. SD, FMS. Military service, World War II.
    Resident, Brunei. Resident commissioner, Gilbert and
    Ellice Islands, 1949-51. Member of Parliament.

Pengilley, Ernest Edgar, b. 1897

  Christ's Hospital. Exeter College, Oxford.

  Military service, World War I. Cadet, FMS, 1921. Malay. SD,
    FMS, UMS. Resident, Brunei. Interned by the Japanese,
    Sarawak. Commissioner of lands, Malaya. Retired 1952.
    Re-employed, settlement work.

Penney, Frederick Gordon

Trinity College, Glenalmond. Edinburgh University. Student, Inner Temple.

Cadet, SS, 1876. Malay. SD, SS. Colonial secretary, 1905.

Pennington, Harold Evelyn, b. 1880

Trinity College, Oxford.

Served in Kelantan (under Siam), 1905-09. Cadet, FMS, 1909. Malay. District posts, FMS, UMS. Killed in action, World War I.

Pepper, John Edward, b. 1903

Nottingham High School. St. John's College, Cambridge.

Cadet, FMS, 1928. Malay. District posts, FMS. Interned by the Japanese. Permanent secretary, ministry of local government and housing. Retired 1957.

Pepys, Walter Evelyn, CMG, 1885-1966

Son of barrister. Malvern College. Brasenose College, Oxford.

Cadet, FMS, 1908. Malay. SD, FMS, SS, UMS. General adviser, Johore. Sarawak. Interned by the Japanese. Retired 1945. See also entries 183, 334.

Pickering, William Alexander, CMG, 1840-1907

Son of agent to coal association. Privately educated in Nottingham.

Merchant sailor, 1862. China Maritime Customs. Commercial employment, Formosa. Chinese interpreter, SS, 1871. Protector of Chinese, 1877. Retired 1889. Wrote report on Sungei Ujong, 1874. See also entries 264, 401.

Portley, William

Clerk, education department, London, 1877. Cadet, SS, 1881. Chinese. Protectorate posts.

Pountney, Arthur Meek, CMG, CBE, 1873-1940

  Reading School. University College, Oxford.

  Cadet, FMS, 1896. Chinese. Protectorate, SD, FMS, SS.
    Financial adviser, SS, FMS. Retired 1926.

Powell, Francis

  Madras College. St. Andrews University.

  Cadet, SS, 1878. Chinese. Protectorate and secretariat
    posts, SS. Protector of Chinese, SS.

Pratt, Edward, b. 1875

  Called to the bar, Middle Temple.

  Cadet, FMS, 1898. Malay. Military service, World War I.
    District posts, FMS, SS, UMS. District officer, Province
    Wellesley. Retired 1930.

Pretty, Eric Ernest Falk, CMG, 1891-1967

  Harrow School. Magdalen College, Oxford.

  Cadet, SS, 1914. Malay. SD, SS, FMS, UMS. Interned by the
    Japanese. British adviser, Johore. Resident, Brunei.
    Retired 1951. Agent for Brunei, London.

Pryde, William, b. 1880

  Edinburgh University. Called to the bar, Lincoln's Inn.

  Cadet, FMS, 1903. Malay. District posts, FMS, UMS, SS.
    Legal adviser, Johore. Retired 1931.

Purcell, Victor William Williams Saunders, CMG, Ph.D., Litt.D.,
  1896-1965

  Bancroft's School. Trinity College, Cambridge.

  Cadet, FMS, 1921. Chinese. Protectorate, SD, FMS, SS, UMS.
    Protector of Chinese, Kedah, Selangor, Pahang. British
    Information Service, United States, 1941. Political duties,
    London and Australia. British Military Administration,
    Malaya, 1945. Retired 1946. Lecturer, Cambridge and United
    States. See also entries 81, 185, 266, 404, 405.

Raja Abdul Aziz bin Raja Muda Musa, b. 1887
  Probationer, 1908. District posts, Perak.

Raja Abdulrahman bin ex-Sultan Abdullah, b. 1882
  Settlement officer, Perak, 1901.

Raja Aman Shah bin Raja Harun, 1902-1942
  Malay College.
  Probationer, 1919. Malay officer. District posts, FMS. MCS
    1933. District officer, Port Dickson.
  Captain, FMS Volunteer Force. Captured and executed by the
    Japanese after the surrender of Singapore.

Raja Haji Abu Bakar bin Raja Omar, b. 1870
  Penghulu, Perak, 1892. District posts, Perak.

Raja Haji Ahmad bin Raja Indut, OBE, b. 1892
  Malay College.
  Malay officer 1913. District posts, FMS. Mentri besar,
    Perlis, 1956-63.

Raja Sir Chulan, KBE, CMG, 1869-1933
  Son of ex-Sultan Abdullah.
  Settlement officer, Perak, 1892. District posts, Perak.
    Retired 1910. Served in the federal council.

Raja Kamaralzaman ibni Raja Mansur, CMG, OBE (also Kamarul-
    zaman), 1892-1962
  Grandson of ex-Sultan Abdullah. Malay College.
  Settlement officer, FMS, 1910. District posts, FMS. Retired
    1947. See also entries 320, 335.

Raja Kechil Tengah Said Tauphy ibni ex-Sultan Abdullah, MBE,
    b. 1879
  Settlement officer, Perak, 1900. District posts, FMS.

Raja Muhammad Mansur bin ex-Sultan Abdullah, b. 1866

Cadet, Perak, 1883. Served on sultan's staff. District posts, Perak.

Raja Musa bin Raja Haji Bot, b. 1897

Malay College. Called to the bar, Inner Temple.

Probationer, 1910. Malay officer. SD, FMS.

Raja Salim bin Raja Mohamed Yusuf, b. 1890

Malay College.

Settlement officer, FMS, 1907. Malay officer. District posts, Perak.

Raja Tun Sir Uda bin Raja Muhammad, KBE, b. 1894

Probationer, FMS, 1910. Malay officer. SD, FMS. Mentri besar, Selangor. Commissioner in London. Speaker, federal council. Governor of Penang, 1957-67.

Ramsay, Arthur Bawtree (Cobden-Ramsay), 1903-1977

Sherborne School. Sidney Sussex College, Cambridge.

Cadet, SS, 1927. Malay. SD, SS, FMS, UMS. Interned by the Japanese. British adviser, Kedah. Retired 1953. See also entries 268, 336.

Raper, Alexander Vincent, b. 1896

Cadet, FMS, 1921. Malay. District posts, FMS.

Rawlings, George Shirley, 1904-1963

Rossall School. Gonville and Caius College, Cambridge.

Cadet, SS, 1929. Malay. Chinese. Protectorate, SD, FMS, SS, UMS. Evacuated from Singapore due to knowledge of Japanese language. British adviser, Kedah. Retired 1959. Killed in road accident, Afghanistan, after serving in West Irian.

Rayman, Lazarus, b. 1889

Manchester Grammar School. Wadham College, Oxford.

Cadet, FMS, 1913. Malay. SD, FMS, SS, UMS. Interned by Japanese. Retired 1945.

Rea, James Taylor, CMG, b. 1907

Son of clergyman. Royal School, Dungannon. Queen's University, Belfast. St. John's College, Cambridge.

Cadet, FMS, 1931. Chinese. Protectorate posts, FMS, SS. Prisoner of war. President, city council, Singapore. Retired 1958.

Reay, James McCabe, b. 1875

Dublin University. Called to the bar, King's Inn.

Cadet, FMS, 1898. Malay. SD, FMS, UMS. Puisne judge, SS.

Reeves, Walter Geoffrey, b. 1906

Bancroft's School. Sidney Sussex College, Cambridge.

Cadet, SS, 1930. Malay. District posts, SS, UMS. Resigned 1938.

Reid, James Stuart Wellesley, OBE, 1899-1972

George Watson's College. Edinburgh University.

Cadet, FMS, 1921. Malay. SD, FMS, SS, UMS. Served in India, World War II. Malayan Establishment Office. Retired 1948.

Rendle, Hilary Cameron Russel, 1899-1944

Son of physician. Christ's College, New Zealand. New College, Oxford.

Cadet, FMS, 1921. Malay. SD, FMS, SS, UMS. Interned by the Japanese. Died following interrogation by Japanese in camp.

Rex, Marcus, CMG, 1886-c.1971

Highgate School. Trinity College, Cambridge.

Cadet, FMS, 1910. Malay. SD, FMS, UMS. Resident, Perak. Retired 1941.

Richards, Daniel, b. 1886

Foyle College, Londonderry. Queen's University, Belfast.

Cadet, FMS, 1910. Chinese. Protectorate, SD, FMS, SS, UMS. Retired 1934.

Richmond, Harold Stedman, b. 1890

Oxford University.

Cadet, FMS, 1913. Killed in action, World War I.

Ridges, Henry Charles, b. 1853

Son of coach builder, Wolverhampton. Trinity College, Cambridge.

Missionary in China. Local appointee, Selangor, 1884. Chinese Protectorate, SD, FMS. Secretary for Chinese Affairs, FMS. Retired 1910.

Rigby, James Philip Clayton, b. 1874

Called to the bar, Lincoln's Inn.

Private secretary to judge, SS, 1897. Malay. District and legal posts, SS, FMS. See also entry 366.

Rigby, William Edward, MC, 1897-1972

Bury Grammar School.

Military service, World War I. Cadet, SS, 1920. Chinese. Protectorate and secretariat posts, SS, FMS. Interned by the Japanese. Retired 1950.

Robertson, G.H. Minot

Cadet, SS, 1908. Chinese. Killed in action, World War I.

Robinson, Franklyn, b. 1878

Dunelm. Called to the bar, Inner Temple.

Cadet, SS, 1903. Malay. SD, SS, FMS, UMS. Acting head, Malay College. Legal adviser, Kedah. Retired 1930.

Robinson, Sir William (C.F.), GCMG, 1835-1897

   Son of admiral. Royal Naval School, Newcross.

   Private secretary to elder brother, Sir Hercules Robinson
      (Lord Rosemead), Colonial Service, 1855-60. Served in West
      Indies. Governor, Falkland Islands; Western Australia; SS,
      1877-79. Governor, Western Australia, 1880; South Australia,
      1882; Western Australia, 1890.

Rodger, Sir John (Pickersgill), KCMG, 1851-1910

   Younger son of Robert Rodger, Hadlow Castle, Kent. Eton Col-
      lege. Christ Church, Oxford.

   Local appointee, Selangor, 1882. District posts, Malay states.
      Resident, Pahang, Selangor, Perak. Retired 1903.

Ross, Alexander Noel, 1905-1972

   St. Andrew's, Grahamstown. Blackfriars School, Northampton.
      Dominican Priory, Woodchester.

   Cadet, FMS, 1930. Malay. District posts, FMS, UMS. Prisoner
      of war. British adviser, Selangor, Kelantan. Retired 1953.
      Wrote Benua vocabulary.

Ross, Edward Andrew, MC, 1895-1975

   Leigh Grammar School. Manchester University.

   Military service, World War I. Cadet, FMS, 1920. Labor. Labor,
      SD, FMS, SS, UMS. Deputy commissioner, Labor. Retired 1947.

Ross, Oswald Bishop, b. 1874

   Manchester University.

   Cadet, SS, 1897. Chinese. Protectorate, SD, SS.

Rowley, Thomas William, b. 1859

   Military service, England and New Zealand. Local appointee,
      Perak, 1889. Malay. District and police posts, FMS.

Samah bin Haji Ali, Dato' Abu, b. 1894

   Malay College.

   Probationer, 1912. Malay officer. District posts, FMS, UMS.
      State secretary, Pahang, 1948.

Saunders, Charles James, b. 1868

  Oxford University.

  Cadet, SS, 1891. Chinese. Protectorate, SD, SS. Secretary
    for Chinese Affairs, SS, FMS. Retired 1923.

Schultz, C.A.

  Local appointee, Perak, 1884. Chinese. Protector of Chinese,
    Perak, 1884-87.

Scott, Sir John, KBE, CMG, 1878-1946

  Son of clergyman. Bath College. King's School, Canterbury.

  Ceylon Civil Service, 1901. Deputy chief secretary, Nigeria,
    1921. Chief secretary, Tanganyika, 1924. Colonial secretary,
    SS, 1929. Retired 1933.

Scott, Ralph, b. 1874

  Cadet, SS, 1895. Malay. SD, SS, FMS. Resident councillor,
    Penang. Retired 1928.

Scott, Walter Dare, b. 1870

  Lieutenant, Lincolnshire Regiment, 1890. Chief clerk, Ulu
    Selangor, 1891. Malay. District posts, FMS, SS, UMS. British
    agent, Trengganu. Acting general adviser, Johore, 1922-23.
    See also entry 270.

Sedwick, Nathaniel Asher, b. 1890

  University College School, London. London University. St.
    Peter's College, Cambridge.

  Cadet, SS, 1913. Malay. SD, SS, UMS. Retired 1935.

Sells, Herbert Cumberlege, b. 1874

  Oxford University.

  Cadet, SS, 1897. Malay. SD, SS, FMS. Secretary for postal
    affairs, SS, FMS. Retired 1929.

Sennett, Cedric William Arthur, b. 1890

Plymouth College. Edinburgh University. Oxford University.

Cadet, SS, 1914. Malay. SD, SS, FMS, UMS. Interned by the
Japanese. Commissioner, lands, Singapore. Retired 1947.

Seth, George Galistaun, King's Counsel, b. 1877

Called to the bar, Gray's Inn.

Cadet, SS, 1901. Malay. SD and legal posts, SS. Solicitor-
general, SS. Retired 1928.

Severn, Sir Claud, KBE, CMG, 1869-1933

Nephew of governor of Bombay. St. Peter's College, Adelaide.
Selwyn College, Cambridge.

Foreign Office, 1891. Private secretary to governor, SS, 1892.
Junior officer, Selangor, 1895. Malay. SD, FMS. Colonial
secretary, SS, 1912. Colonial secretary, Hong Kong, 1912.
Retired 1926.

Shaw, Edward Wingfield, d. 1879

Captain, Royal Navy. Private secretary to governor, Antigua,
1863. Administrator, Monserrat, 1865-66. Lieutenant-governor,
Malacca, 1968. Died in service, 1879.

Shaw, George Ernest, CMG, OBE, 1877-1958

Dublin University (B.A., LL.B.).

Cadet, FMS, 1900. Malay. SD, FMS, SS, UMS. General adviser,
Johore. Retired 1931.

Sheehan, John Joseph, 1896-1945

Christian Schools, Dublin. University College, Dublin.

Cadet, FMS, 1920. Malay. SD, FMS, UMS. Interned by the Japanese. Died immediately after liberation.

Shelley, Malcolm Bond, CMG, 1879-1968

Dulwich College. Christ's College, Cambridge.

Cadet, FMS, 1902. Labor. Labor, SD, FMS, SS. Chief secretary,
FMS. Retired 1935. Wrote on bankruptcy law.

Sheppard, Mervyn Cecil ffrank, CMG, MBE (Tan Sri Datuk Haji
    Abdul Mubin Sheppard), b. 1905

  Son of clergyman. Marlborough College. Magdalene College,
    Cambridge.

  Cadet, FMS, 1927. Malay. SD, FMS, UMS. Interned by the
    Japanese. British adviser, Negri Sembilan. Head, emergency
    (insurrection) food denial organization. Keeper of public
    records and director of museums. Retired 1958. See also
    entries 86, 87, 88, 271, 272, 273, 344, 345, 346, 347,
    348, 349.

Sherwood, Montague Earle, MBE, b. 1884

  Pocklington School. Magdalen College, Oxford.

  Cadet, SS, 1907. Malay. SD, SS.

Shorland, Christopher William, b. 1902

  Son of clergyman. Wellington College. Exeter College, Oxford.
    Called to the bar, Inner Temple.

  Cadet, FMS, 1924. Labor. Labor, SD, FMS, SS, UMS. Interned
    by the Japanese. District officer, Kinta. Retired 1951.

Simmons, James William, b. 1877

  Oxford University.

  Cadet, FMS, 1900. Malay. SD, FMS, SS, UMS. Resident, Selangor.
    Retired 1932.

Simpson-Gray, Lester Cartwright, b. 1904

  Winchester College. New College, Oxford. Called to the bar,
    Middle Temple.

  Cadet, FMS, 1926. Labor. Labor and legal posts, FMS, UMS,
    SS. Missing in action, World War II.

Sircom, Harold Sebastian, b. 1878

  M.A., Victoria, Manchester.

  Cadet, FMS, 1902. Malay. SD, FMS, SS, UMS. Controller of
    rubber, SS, FMS. Retired 1927.

Skinner, Allan Maclean, CMG, 1846-1901

Son of judge. Called to the bar, Lincoln's Inn.

Cadet, SS, 1868. Malay. SD, SS. Resident councillor, Penang. Retired 1897. Founder of *SBRAS*. Wrote on geography. See also entries 90, 274.

Skinner, Charles James

Cadet, SS, 1876. SD, SS, Perak. Retired 1889.

Sleep, Arthur, CMG, 1894-1959

Ulverston Grammar School. Manchester University.

Cadet, FMS, 1920. Malay. SD, FMS, UMS. Interned by the Japanese. British adviser, Johore. Retired 1949.

Small, Sir Alexander (Sym), KBE, CMG, 1887-1944

Dalziel High School. Glasgow University.

Cadet, FMS, 1911. Malay. SD, FMS, SS, UMS. Colonial secretary, SS. Retired 1940.

Smith, Sir Cecil Clementi, GCMG, 1840-1916

Son of clergyman. St. Paul's School. Corpus Christi College, Cambridge.

Cadet, Hong Kong, 1862. Colonial secretary, SS, 1878. Lieutenant-governor and colonial secretary, Ceylon, 1885. Governor, SS, 1887. Retired 1893. Wrote booklet criticizing Sir Frank Swettenham's *British Malaya*.

Smith, Christopher Patrick, b. 1894

Cadet, FMS, 1921. Chinese. Protectorate posts, FMS. Retired 1933.

Smith, Gerald Archibald John (Smith-Steinmetz), b. 1878

Called to the bar, Middle Temple.

Cadet, SS, 1902. Labor. Labor, SD, SS, FMS.

Smith, James David Maxwell, CMG, 1895-1969

  Robert Gordon's College. Aberdeen University.

  Cadet, FMS, 1920. Malay. SD, FMS, UMS. Interned by the
    Japanese. Financial secretary, Singapore. Retired 1951.
    United Nations, Latin America.

Somerville, David Alford, 1908-1974

  Son of clergyman. King's School, Canterbury. Corpus Christi
    College, Cambridge.

  Cadet, FMS, 1932. Malay. SD, FMS, UMS. Naval intelligence,
    Australia and India, during World War II. British adviser,
    Johore. Retired 1957.

Speedy, Tristram Charles Sawyer, 1836-1910

  Son of Indian army officer.

  Served in New Zealand militia, in Ethopia and in Indian police
    Superintendent of police, Penang, 1871. Employed by mentri
    of Larut to recruit sepoys, 1873. Assistant resident,
    Perak, 1874. Resigned 1877.

Sproule, Percy Julian, b. 1873

  Cambridge University. Called to the bar, Middle Temple.

  Cadet, SS, 1895. Chinese. Secretariat and legal posts, SS,
    FMS. Puisne judge. Retired 1932.

Stark, Walter John Kirkpatrick, OBE, b. 1887

  Aberdeen University.

  Cadet, FMS, 1910. Labor. Labor, SD, FMS, SS. Retired 1933.
    Re-employed as immigration agent in India. Retired 1947.
    See also entry 275.

Staynes, George Francis, b. 1906

  Bradford Grammar School. Hertford College, Oxford.

  Cadet, SS, 1930. Malay. District and co-operatives posts, FMS,
    SS, UMS. Prisoner of war. Died in camp.

Stevens, Frederick Guy, b. 1878

  Oxford University.

  Cadet, SS, 1902. Wrote on registration of deeds.

Stevens, Harry Hastings, b. 1890

  Cambridge University.

  Cadet, FMS, 1913. Resigned 1921.

Stirling, William George, b. 1887

  Assistant superintendent, government monopolies, Malacca,
    1909. Protectorate and secretariat posts, SS, FMS. Extra
    assistant protector of Chinese, 1921. See also entries 409,
    410, 411, 419.

Stoney, Bowes Ormonde, b. 1878

  Cadet, FMS, 1902. Malay. District posts, FMS.

Stonor, Oswald Francis Gerald, CMG, 1872-1940

  Son of justice of the peace. Oscot. Stonyhurst.

  Acting private secretary to the governor, SS, 1890. Junior
    officer, Selangor, 1890. Malay. SD, FMS. Resident, Selangor,
    Perak. Retired 1926.

Stratton, George Bernard, b. 1876

  Cadet, SS, 1899. Malay. SD, SS. Resigned 1911.

Sturrock, Alfred John, b. 1879

  Edinburgh University.

  Cadet, FMS, 1902. Malay. SD, FMS, UMS. British adviser,
    Trengganu. Retired 1931. Wrote, with Winstedt, four Malay
    texts.

Sugars, John Charles, b. 1875

Dublin University. Barrister.

Cadet, FMS, 1898. Malay. SD, FMS, SS, UMS. Acting solicitor-general, SS.

Swettenham, Sir Alexander, KCMG, 1846-1933

Son of solicitor. Clare College, Cambridge.

Ceylon Civil Service, 1868. Receiver-general, Cyprus, 1884. Auditor-general, Ceylon, 1891. Colonial secretary, SS, 1895. Acting governor, 1898, 1899-1901 (and acting high commissioner, Malay states). Governor, British Guiana, 1901. Jamaica, 1904. Retired 1907.

Swettenham, Sir Frank (Athelstane), CH, GCMG, 1850-1946

Son of solicitor. St. Peter's School, York.

Cadet, SS, 1870. Malay. SD, SS, Malay states. Resident, Selangor, Perak. Resident-general, FMS. Governor, SS and high commissioner, Malay states. Retired 1904. See also entries 190, 191, 278, 279, 280, 352, 353, 354, 355, 356, 357, 358.

Syed Noordin bin Syed Hussein, b. 1901

Malay College.

Probationer, 1920. Malay officer. District posts, FMS. MCS 1947. District officer, Kuala Lumpur, Telok Anson. Retired 1952.

Sykes, George Rognvald, b. 1889

Birkenhead School. Liverpool University.

Cadet, SS, 1913. Chinese. Protectorate and secretariat posts, SS, FMS, UMS. Commissioner, trade and customs, Johore. Retired 1940.

Talbot, Arthur Philip

Haileybury. Trinity College, Cambridge.

Cadet, SS, 1874. Malay. SD, SS, Malay states. Assistant colonial secretary, SS, 1893.

Talma, Edwy Lyonet, b. 1874

  Cambridge University. Called to the bar, Inner Temple.

  Cadet, SS, 1896. Labor. Labor, secretariat and legal posts,
    SS.

Tatham, W.T.

  Captain, Royal Artillery.

  Temporary assistant resident, Sungei Ujong, 1874. Retired
    for health reasons, 1875.

Taylor, Evan Nuttall, b. 1898

  Called to the bar.

  Military service, World War I. Cadet, FMS, 1921. Malay.
    SD, FMS. Transferred to colonial legal service. Interned
    by the Japanese. Puisne judge, Singapore. Retired 1956.
    See also entry 359.

Taylor, Frederick Edward, b. 1877

  Trinity College, Cambridge.

  Cadet, FMS, 1900. Malay. SD, FMS, UMS. Retired 1924.

Taylor, William Cecil, b. 1902

  Bolton School. Manchester University. LL.B. Solicitor of the
    Supreme Court of England.

  Cadet, SS, 1924. Malay. District, protectorate and legal posts,
    SS, UMS. Served in Nigeria during World War II. Financial
    secretary, Singapore. Retired 1954.

Taylor, Sir William (Thomas), KCMG, 1848-1931

  Civil service, Cyprus, 1879-91. Auditor, Ceylon, 1895-1901.
    Colonial secretary, SS, 1902-04. Resident-general, FMS,
    1905. Retired 1910. Head of Malay States Information Agency,
    London.

Thomas, Sir (Thomas) Shenton (Whitelegge), GCMG, OBE, 1879-1962

  Son of clergyman. St. John's School, Leatherhead. Queens'
    College, Cambridge.

Colonial service, East African Protectorate, 1909. Uganda.
Nigeria. Colonial secretary, Gold Coast, 1927. Governor,
Nyasaland, 1929. Gold Coast, 1932. SS (and high commissioner
Malay states), 1934. Interned by the Japanese. Retired
1946. See also entry 195.

Thompson, Henry Arthur

Royal School, Armagh. Dublin University.

Cadet, SS, 1881. Labor. Died from tuberculosis, 1889.

Thompson, Sir Robert (Grainger Ker), KBE, CMG, Distinguished
Service Order, MC, b. 1916

Son of clergyman. Marlborough College. Sidney Sussex College,
Cambridge.

MCS, 1938. Royal Air Force, 1941-46. Staff posts during
insurrection in Malaya. Permanent secretary, ministry of
defense, 1959. Retired 1961. Head, British advisory mission.
Vietnam, 1961-65. Wrote on communist insurgency. See also
entry 452.

Thomson, Henry Wagstaffe, CMG, 1874-1941

Winchester College. Trinity College, Oxford.

Cadet, FMS, 1896. Malay. SD, FMS, SS, UMS. Britsh adviser,
Kalantan. Resident, Pahang, Perak. Served in Siamese Civil
Service, 1906-09. Retired 1929.

Thorogood, William Jesse, MC, b. 1896

Latymer Upper School. Trinity College, Cambridge.

Cadet, FMS, 1921. Labor. Labor and district posts, FMS, SS,
UMS. Transferred to colonial legal service. On leave in
England during World War II. Registrar, Supreme Court. Re-
tired 1949.

Thorold, Frederick Thorold

Wellington College. Stuttgart University.

"Cadet," Perak, 1886. District posts. Resigned 1897.

Tickell, George Templer, b. 1858

Cheltenham College.

Served in Australian survey department, the China Maritime Customs and the North Borneo service. District engineer, Perak, 1884. District posts, Selangor. Resigned 1890. Appointed president, sanitary board, Kuala Lumpur, 1902. See also entry 281.

Townley, Edmund Francis, b. 1866

Mines department, Pahang, 1890. District posts, Pahang and Selangor.

Tranchell, Edward Charles John, b. 1863

Barmter Court School, Southampton.

Local appointee, Perak, 1885. District posts, Perak, Selangor. Assistant district officer, Kuala Lipis. Retired 1905.

Treacher, Sir William (Hood), KCMG, 1849-1919

Son of clergyman. Oxford University.

Local appointee, Labuan, 1871. Colonial secretary, 1887. Governor, North Borneo, 1881. Secretary to government, Perak, 1888. Resident, Selangor, Perak. Resident-general, FMS, 1902. Retired 1904. See also entries 93, 198.

Tree, Francis Thomas, b. 1887

Diocesan College, Dublin. Trinity College, Dublin.

Military service, World War I. Cadet, FMS, 1910. Malay. SD, FMS, SS, UMS. Retired 1935.

Trevenen, N.P.

Cadet, SS, 1874. Chinese. Protectorate, SD, SS, Malay states. Consul, Brunei, Sarawak and North Borneo, 1890.

Turnbull, Sir Ronald (Evelyn), KCMG, 1905-c.1962

  King's College, London. St. John's College, Oxford.

  Cadet, FMS, 1929. Malay. SD, FMS, SS, UMS. Colonial Office,
    1937. Singapore, 1939. Colonial secretary, British Honduras,
    1940. War Office, 1943-45. High commission territories,
    1950. Governor, North Borneo, 1954.

Turner, Guy Elliot, b. 1907

  Son of officer in Indian Civil Service. Haileybury College.
    St. John's College, Cambridge.

  Cadet, FMS, 1931. Labor. Labor and district posts, FMS, SS.
    Interned by the Japanese. Deputy commissioner of labor,
    Perak. Retired 1957. See also entries 415, 416, 417.

Turner, Harold Goodhew, CMG, b. 1906

  St. Olave's School. St. Saviour's Grammar School. Trinity
    College, Cambridge.

  Cadet, FMS, 1929. Malay. SD, FMS, SS, UMS. Interned by the
    Japanese. Malayan Establishment officer. Secretary to the
    treasury, Malaya. Retired 1961. Lecturer, Royal Institute
    of International Affairs. Foreign and Commonwealth Office.
    Director of studies, Royal Institute of Public Administra-
    tion. Retired 1973. See also entry 283.

Turner, Robert Noel, Datuk, CMG, b. 1912

  Son of admiral. Dover College. Wadham College, Oxford.

  Cadet, 1935. Malay. SD, FMS. Interned by the Japanese.
    Sarawak. Malayan Establishment Office. Colonial secretary,
    Barbados, 1950. North Borneo, 1956. Retired 1963.

Turney, C.H.A.

  Clerk, Labuan. Local appointee, Selangor, 1875. SD, Selangor.
    Senior district officer and assistant protector of Indian
    immigrants, 1891.

Valpy, George Cordy, b. 1877

  Christ's College, Cambridge.

  Cadet, FMS, 1901. Chinese. Protectorate, SD, FMS, SS. Retired
    1925.

Vane, Henry George Bagnall, b. 1861

Marlborough College.

Local appointee, assistant auditor, Perak, 1884. Treasurer, FMS, 1914.

Venables, Oswald Eric, 1891-1960

Campbell College. Trinity College, Dublin.

Cadet, SS, 1914. Military service, World War I. SD, SS, FMS, UMS. Interned by the Japanese. Resident commissioner, Kedah. Retired 1948.

Venning, Alfred Reid, b. 1846

Planter in Ceylon. Treasurer, Selangor, 1884. Federal secretary, FMS, 1903.

Vlieland, Charles Archibald, b. 1890

Son of physician. Exeter School. Balliol College, Oxford.

Cadet, FMS, 1914. Malay. SD, FMS, SS, UMS. Secretary for defense, Malaya. Retired 1941. See also entries 101, 201, 456.

Voules, Arthur Blennerhassett, b. 1870

Dulwich College. Sidney Sussex College, Cambridge. Called to the bar, Inner Temple.

Junior officer, Perak, 1892. Malay. SD, FMS, SS. Resident councillor, Penang. Retired 1925.

Walker, George Antony Gilbert, 1909-1943

Son of general. Rugby School. Oriel College, Oxford.

Cadet, SS, 1932. Malay. SD, SS, UMS. Interned by the Japanese. Died in camp.

Walker, Henry James Noel, b. 1872

Son of Sir Edward Walker. Cambridge University.

Junior officer, Perak, 1896. Malay. SD, FMS.

Walker, Lt. Col. Robert Sandilands Frowd, CMG, Fellow of the
Royal Geographical Society, 1850-1917

Royal Military Academy, Sandhurst.

Acting commissioner, Perak Armed Police, 1879. Acting resident, Perak and Selangor. Commandant, Malay States Guides.

Wall, Alfred Henry

Clifton College.

Local appointee, Selangor public works department, 1886.
District posts, Pahang.

Walton, Bryan Stagg, b. 1899

Berkhamsted School. Pembroke College, Oxford.

Cadet, SS, 1913. Malay. Military service, World War I. SD,
SS, FMS, UMS. Retired 1939.

Wan Muhammad Isa bin Ibrahim, Orang Kaya Mentri, b. 1866

Penghulu, Perak, 1890. District posts, Perak.

Wan Muhammad Salleh, Orang Kaya Kaya Sri Adika Raja, b. 1861

Penghulu, Perak, 1880. District posts, Perak.

Ward, Norman, b. 1904

Bradford Grammar School. Queen's College, Oxford.

Cadet, SS, 1928. Malay. District posts, SS, UMS. Interned
by the Japanese. Deputy chief secretary, Malaya. Retired
1957.

Ward, Robert Adrian, 1912-1942

Sherborne School. Hertford College, Oxford.

Cadet, 1935. Malay. District posts, SS, UMS. Re-entered Johore
after Japanese conquest. Killed in action.

Ward, Wilfred Arthur, CMG, MC, b. 1892

Christ's Hospital.

Military service, World War I. Cadet, FMS, 1920. Malay. SD, FMS, UMS. Under-secretary, SS, 1941. Interned by the Japanese. Commissioner for Malaya, United Kingdom. Retired 1953.

Watherston, Sir David (Charles), KBE, CMG, 1907-1977

Westminster School. Christ Church, Oxford.

Cadet, FMS, 1930. Malay. SD, FMS. Malay Establishment Office. Colonial Office, 1939-44. Chief secretary, Malaya. Retired 1957. Counsellor to Malayan high commissioner, London, 1957-59.

Watson, Henry, 1909-1945

Son of clergyman. Campbell College, Belfast. Trinity College, Dublin.

Cadet, 1934. Labor. Labor and secretariat posts, SS, FMS. Prisoner of war. Shot by the Japanese, Labuan.

Watson, Reginald George, CMG, 1862-1926

Son of general. Haileybury.

Cadet, SS, 1883. Chinese. Protectorate, SD, SS, FMS. Federal secretary. Resident, Perak. Retired 1919.

Watts, E.H.

Cadet, SS, 1870.

Webb, George William, 1904-1974

University College, London.

Cadet, FMS, 1928. Chinese. Protectorate, SD, SS, FMS. Interned by the Japanese. Secretary, Chinese Affairs, Singapore, Selangor. Retired 1957.

Weisberg, Hyman, CMG, 1890-c.1977

Central Foundation School, London. Christ's College, Cambridge.

Cadet, FMS, 1914. Malay. SD, FMS, SS. Financial secretary, SS. Allied commission, Austria, 1946. Foreign Office, London, 1947. See also entry 285.

Weld, Sir Frederick (Aloysius), KCMG, 1823-1891

Grandson of 6th Lord Clifford of Chudleigh. Stonyhurst. Freiburg.

Farmed in New Zealand. Ministerial appointments. Governor, Western Australia, 1869. Tasmania, 1874. SS, 1880-87. See also entry 103.

Weld, Frederick Joseph, b. 1870

Son of Sir Frederick Weld.

Junior officer, Perak, 1888. Malay. District and state posts, Malay states. Acting resident, Pahang, 1914.

Welman, Gerard Wilfrid

Local appointee, Perak, 1883. District and state posts, Perak and Selangor. Retired c. 1903.

White, H.F. Coghlan

Local appointee, Perak, 1886. District posts.

Whitehouse, Bertram Reginald, b. 1891

King Edward's School, Birmingham. St. John's College, Cambridge.

Military service, World War I. Cadet, SS, 1915. Malay. SD, SS, UMS. District judge, SS. Retired 1935.

Whitley, Sir Michael Henry, Kt., 1872-1959

Son of gentleman, Surrey. Blundell's School. King's College, London. Called to the bar, Inner Temple.

Junior officer, FMS, 1896. Malay. SD, SS, FMS, UMS. Attorney-general, SS. Retired 1929.

Whitton, Cuthbert Henry, b. 1905

St. Andrew's College, Dublin. Trinity College, Dublin.

Cadet, SS, 1929. Malay. Transferred to colonial legal service. Interned by the Japanese. Retired 1957. See also entry 286.

Wilkinson, Richard James, CMG, 1867–1941

Son of consular official. Cambridge University.

Cadet, SS, 1889. Malay and Chinese. SD, SS, FMS. Inspector of schools, FMS. Colonial secretary, SS, 1911–16. Governor, Sierra Leone, 1916–22. See also entries 361, 362, 363, 364, 365, 366, 367, 368, 373.

Willan, Sir Harold (Curwen), Kt., CMG, MC, 1896–c.1973

Kendal Grammar School. Jesus College, Oxford. Called to the bar, Inner Temple.

Cadet, FMS, 1920. Malay. District posts, SS, FMS. Transferred to colonial legal service. Solicitor-general, Kenya, 1937. Zanzibar. Chief justice, Malaya, 1946 and 1948–50. High commission territories, 1952–56.

Williams, Arthur, b. 1899

Wade Deacon Grammar School, Widnes. London University. Called to the bar, Middle Temple.

Naval service, World War I. Cadet, SS, 1924. Malay. SD, SS, UMS. Interned by the Japanese. Financial secretary, Singapore. Retired 1949.

Williams, Edward Bridgewater, b. 1885

Wellington College.

Cadet, FMS, 1908. Malay. SD, FMS, UMS. Acting legal adviser, FMS. Retired 1939. Wrote report of committee on bankruptcy legislation.

Williams, Eric Tregear, 1890–1972

Blundell's School. Balliol College, Oxford.

Cadet, SS, 1913. Malay. SD, SS, FMS, UMS. Under-secretary, SS. Retired 1941.

Williams, Frank Leslie, 1899–1943

  Son of army officer. Weymouth College. Christ's College, Cambridge.

  Cadet, FMS, 1921. Chinese. Protectorate posts, FMS, UMS. Prisoner of war. Died in Thailand.

Williams, Philip Stanhope, b. 1889

  Harrow School. Gonville and Caius College, Cambridge.

  Cadet, FMS, 1912. Malay. SD, FMS, UMS, SS. Retired 1937.

Wills, Daniel, 1898–1946

  King's School, Rochester. Royal Military College, Sandhurst.

  Cadet, SS, 1921. Malay. SD, SS, UMS. Interned by the Japanese. Retired 1946.

Wilson, Charles, 1889–1966

  Foyle College, Derry. Trinity College, Dublin. Called to the bar, King's Inn.

  Cadet, FMS, 1913. Labor. Labor, SD, FMS, SS. Controller of labor, Malaya. Retired for health reasons, 1941. See also entry 420.

Wilson, Frank Kershaw, 1891–1976

  Bradford Grammar School. Brasenose College, Oxford.

  Cadet, SS, 1914. Malay. SD, SS, FMS, UMS. Interned by the Japanese. Retired 1945.

Wilson, George Gordon, b. 1876

  Aberdeen University.

  Cadet, SS, 1899. Chinese. Secretariat posts, SS. Acting postmaster-general, SS.

Wilson, Ronald Eric, 1898–1961

  Faversham. Royal Military College, Sandhurst.

  Cadet, FMS, 1921. Malay. SD, FMS, UMS. Retired 1940.

Winnington-Ingram, Eric Alfred, b. 1902

Cadet, SS, 1925. Malay. District posts, SS. Retired 1932.

Winstedt, Sir Richard (Olaf), KBE, CMG, D.Litt., 1878-1966

Magdalen College School. New College, Oxford.

Cadet, FMS, 1902. Malay. SD, educational posts, FMS, SS.
Director of education, SS and FMS. General adviser, Johore.
Retired 1935. Reader in Malay, London University. See also
entries 108, 109, 110, 202, 287, 288, 289, 369, 370, 371,
372, 373.

Wise, Dacres Hope

Son of army officer. Marlborough College.

"Cadet," Perak, 1885. District and state posts, Malay states.

Wise, Edward Ashton

Son of army officer. HMS Britannia. Sherborne College.

Local appointee, Pahang, 1889. District posts, Pahang. Killed
in Pahang disturbances, 1894.

Wolferston, Littleton Edward Pipe, b. 1866

Eton College. Clare College, Cambridge.

Cadet, SS, 1889. Malay. SD, SS. Resident councillor, Malacca.
Retired 1922.

Wolff, Ernest Charteris Holford, CMG, 1875-1946

Merchiston Castle School, Edinburgh. Trinity College, Oxford.

Cadet, FMS, 1897. Malay. SD, FMS, SS, UMS. Resident, Negri
Sembilan. Retired 1928.

Wolters, O.W., OBE, Ph.D., b. 1915

Oxford University.

Cadet, 1937. Chinese. Prisoner of war. In charge of resettling
Chinese in new villages. Retired 1957. Lecturer, School
of Oriental and African Studies, London University. Professor of history, Cornell University.

Wood, William Harold, b. 1896

  Military service, World War I. Cadet, FMS, 1921. Malay.
    District posts, FMS, UMS.

Woodward, Sir Lionel (Mabbott), Kt. Bach., 1864-1925

  Harrow School. Trinity College, Cambridge. Called to the bar,
    Inner Temple.

  Cadet, SS, 1888. Labor. Labor, SD, SS, FMS. Legal posts.
    Chief justice, FMS, 1921-25.

Worley, Sir Newnham (Arthur), Kt., KBE, 1892-c.1977

  Reigate Grammar School. Emmanuel College, Cambridge. Called
    to the bar, Inner Temple.

  Cadet, FMS, 1914. Chinese. Protectorate, labor and secretariat
    posts, FMS, SS. Transferred to colonial legal service. In-
    terned by the Japanese. Chief justice, British Guiana,
    1947. East African Court of Appeal, 1955. Bermuda, 1958.
    Retired 1960.

Worthington, Arthur Furley, b. 1874

  Cambridge University.

  Cadet, FMS, 1897. Malay. District posts, FMS. British adviser,
    Kelantan. Resident, Perak. Retired 1929.

Wray, Cecil, b. 1850

  Inspector, public works department, Perak, 1881. District
    posts, Perak and Selangor. Resident, Pahang. Retired 1908.
    Wrote account of expedition to Perak mountains, 1887.

Wray, George Crofton

  Haileybury.

  Cadet, SS, 1881. Chinese. Protectorate and district posts,
    SS.

Wright, Alan Austin, b. 1889

Oxford University.

Cadet, FMS, 1912. Killed in action, World War I.

Wyatt, Edward Warren Nevile, b. 1879

Cadet, FMS, 1903. Malay. SD, FMS. Acting British adviser, Perlis. Retired 1927.

York, Arthur Desmond, b. 1907

King's Hospital School, Dublin. Trinity College, Dublin.

Cadet, SS, 1929. Malay. SD, SS, FMS, UMS. Interned by the Japanese. President, municipal commissioners, Kuala Lumpur. Retired 1962.

Young, Capt. Sir Arthur (Henderson), GCMG, KBE, 1854-1938

Son of army officer. Edinburgh Academy. Rugby School. Royal Military College, Sandhurst.

Military service. Police, Cyprus, 1878. Civil service, Cyprus. Colonial secretary, SS, 1906. Chief secretary, FMS, 1911. Governor, SS, and high commissioner, Malay states, 1911-19.

Young, W.M., CBE

Cadet, 1939. Labor. Interned by the Japanese. Deputy secretary, federal treasury. Retired 1960.

SUBJECT INDEX

AUTHOR INDEX

016.9595

H595

114 322